Happy birthday &

happy gardening

Pauline & Ian x x

15 September 2019.

HEAD GARDENERS

HEAD GARDENERS

Ambra Edwards

Photographs by Charlie Hopkinson

AMBRA EDWARDS is a journalist who specializes
in garden history, contemporary garden design and
community gardening. She has three times been
awarded the title of Garden Journalist of the Year by
the Garden Media Guild.

CHARLIE HOPKINSON is a photographer specializing
in portraits, gardening and landscape, and the arts.

Pimpernel Press Limited
www.pimpernelpress.com

Head Gardeners
© Pimpernel Press Limited 2017
Text © Ambra Edwards 2017
Photographs © Charlie Hopkinson 2017
Design by Becky Clarke Design

A catalogue record for this book is available from the British Library.

Typeset in Centaur MT

ISBN 978-1-910258-74-3
Printed and bound in China
by C&C Offset Printing Company Limited

9 8 7 6 5 4 3 2

CONTENTS

ON BEHALF
OF GARDENERS

*'It's difficult to imagine a class of people who have such
tremendous skills, who contribute so much to society,
and who are so thoroughly undervalued.'*

MIKE CALNAN, HEAD OF GARDENS, NATIONAL TRUST

What is Britain's greatest contribution to world culture? I suggest it is the garden. It is an art form we have made peculiarly our own, and which we have been exporting to the rest of the world for at least the last three centuries.

It expresses important ideas about what we value, what we believe in, what we dream of, and what we think is beautiful. It is also an important economic contributor: Britain's great gardens bring in visitors from all over the world. Kew, for example, attracts more visitors than Stonehenge, Westminster Abbey or the Houses of Parliament.[1]

Gardens are hugely important to us. Yet by their very nature they are mutable, making them at once more interesting, and more fragile, than other forms of art. What makes them — and keeps them — special is the input of the people who look after them. These are the head gardeners.

If these highly skilled people, who contribute so much to the pleasure and delight of so many, were singers or footballers, they would earn vast sums and frolic weekly through the pages of celebrity magazines. Yet with a very few exceptions, we don't know who they are.

This book is an attempt to find out, exploring something of the lives, vision and achievement of a range of very different gardeners. Most of them work in well-known and widely visited gardens. Others are intensely and necessarily private. All seem to share an extraordinary energy, born of a passion for

Mick Evans of Packwood House is typical of head gardeners in his anxiety to shun the limelight.

---

1   Association of Leading Visitor Attractions (ALVA) visitor figures, 2014.

their work, and an intelligence, diligence and eye for detail that is humbling to a slipshod amateur gardener like me. And there all resemblance ends, for their understanding of who they are and what they are for could scarcely be more different: today's head gardener may be variously a project manager, conservationist, artist, historian, plantsman, educator, scientific investigator, social worker, public relations supremo, events planner and businessman. Or any combination of the above. And somehow they find time to grow things, too . . .

So how is it that the role of head gardener is not more widely celebrated? These days it is the garden designers who rule the horticultural roost – no mere gardener can command anything like the attention or remuneration. Indeed, the practice of gardening is widely dismissed as a career for the intellectually challenged, or at best a safe haven for the dyslexic, dyspraxic, emotionally fragile or lacking in aspiration. This is curious, because every successful garden requires at least three distinct and highly developed skills. First comes the organization of the space – the cardinal skill of the garden designer. Yet if we look back into history, the greatest masters of this art, in very different idioms, were first head gardeners. In seventeenth-century France, André Le Nôtre, head gardener to Louis XIV, raised the manipulation of geometry and optics in the formal garden into the supreme expression of wealth and political power. On this side of the Channel, the landscape parks of Lancelot 'Capability' Brown, who developed his craft as head gardener at Stowe, came to define some essential quality of Englishness, and to shape what we now think of as natural beauty. No small achievements for 'mere' gardeners.

Next comes plantsmanship – furnishing and enriching the designed space with appropriate planting, a skill that requires both visual artistry and technical knowledge. And this morphs into the craft of gardening, without which no garden can survive. The first two skills perish without the third – it is the skilled technician who brings the designer's vision to fruition, who makes it sing, and then refines and adapts it over months and years. To do this requires forethought, judgement, responsiveness – what garden writer Stephen Switzer, as long ago as 1727, characterized as 'labour of the brain'. [2]

We live in an age that values labour of the brain more highly than labour of the hand. Yet in the case of the sculptor, the painter, the concert pianist or the master chef, we acknowledge that the two are indivisible, that artistry and manual skill go quite literally hand in hand. In what way is it different for a gardener? If we can revere an Anthony Caro or a David Hockney or a Heston

---

2 *The Practical Kitchen Gardiner*, 1727. Quoted by Martin Hoyles, *Bread and Roses*, Pluto Press, 1995, 115.

Blumenthal, it stands to reason we should recognize the no less extraordinary skill of a Mick Evans or a Fergus Garrett. So this book is a shout on behalf of an astonishing cohort of creative spirits too modest, or too busy, to shout for themselves.

———◦◦———

Working gardeners are rarely identified or even acknowledged in the historical record, though clearly there could be no gardens without them. The first documented gardens, the imperial and scholars' gardens of China, appear to have been made by small groups of craftsmen – the Rockery-Men's Guild, Flower-Garden-Men's Guild and the Masters of Hill Building. In the gardens of ancient Rome, a *topiarius* maintained the ornamental garden, as distinct from the orchard or vegetable plot, and letters and tomb inscriptions suggest that his skill was held in high regard.[3] In the monasteries of medieval Europe, monks tended extensive productive and medicinal gardens serving large communities, not dissimilar, in a way, from the garden teams of the Edwardian country house.

Not until the seventeenth century do we see people we would recognize as head gardeners today: plant hunters John Tradescant the Elder and Younger (employed in turn by Queen Henrietta Maria); André and Gabriel Mollet (engaged by Charles II at Hampton Court), their successor John Rose;[4] London and Wise (head gardeners respectively to the Bishop of London and Queen Anne); and, not least Capability Brown, who lobbied hard to become head gardener to George III.

There is a curious notion that the landscape parks of the eighteenth century went ungardened – that with just a modicum of tree work and the odd flock of sheep, they looked after themselves. That is not so: fifty men were employed at Stourhead, while Thomas Jefferson, visiting in 1786, observed fifteen men and eighteen boys at work at Stowe and no fewer than two hundred at Blenheim, where the turf was mowed every ten days.[5] We now know that much more use was made of flowers than previously supposed.[6]

PAGES 12–13 *Behind the scenes at Great Dixter, a reserve supply of annuals that won't be needed as gap-fillers cheerfully flowers unseen.*

3 Linda Farrar, *Ancient Roman Gardens*, Sutton Publishing, 1998, 161–2.
4 A famous painting in the Royal Collection, *Charles II Presented with a Pineapple*, depicts Rose presenting his sovereign with what is said (erroneously) to have been the first pineapple grown in Britain – conceived as the gardener's supreme achievement. It is believed to have been painted to commemorate Rose's death in 1677.
5 Hoyles, *Bread and Roses*, 116.
6 Mark Laird, *The Flowering of the Landscape Garden: English Pleasure Grounds 1720–1800*, Penn Press, 1999.

Brown's plant list for Petworth, for example, is extensive. Meanwhile, the necessary production of fruit and vegetables for the mansion continued in a series of ever more splendid walled gardens. Presiding over the Chelsea Physic Garden, the indefatigable plant collector Philip Miller published the first comprehensive garden dictionary in English in 1731. Asked to recommend a head gardener for Princess Augusta, he sent her William Aiton, who would become the first superintendent of Kew.

But it was in the nineteenth century that the head gardener reached his apogee. He (always he) became a man of substance, highly respected if not generously paid. The best known among them, Joseph Paxton, rose from humble gardener's boy to rub shoulders with the greatest in the land, becoming a knight of the realm, MP, railway magnate and media mogul, and, famously, designer of the Crystal Palace. Others, such as Donald Beaton of Shrubland Hall, Suffolk, and John Caie, gardener to the Duke of Bedford at Bedford Lodge, Kensington, were the Monty Dons and Alan Titchmarshes of their day, penning best-selling books and forming gardening taste by their writings in the new gardening magazines. They were figures of power and influence at the estates where they worked – P. G. Wodehouse's Mr McAllister, who rules the roost at Blandings Castle, is not so very far removed from the truth.

The head gardener's new kudos was the result of profound social change.

At the end of the eighteenth century, the landed aristocracy consisted of some three hundred families, whose wealth and very substantial influence derived from the land. Fifty years on, the picture had changed entirely. Propelled by the Industrial Revolution, it was industry and commerce that were now the principal engines of wealth; a new middle class was enjoying both affluence and increasing political clout; and the expansion of the British Empire, along with a series of technological advances, had wrought dramatic changes in taste.

Paradoxically, the aim of the newly wealthy was overwhelmingly to establish themselves among the landed gentry, giving rise to a frenzy of country house building. But the houses to which they aspired were no longer Palladian mansions afloat on a sea of rolling greensward, but generally more eclectic and highly decorated affairs. Rather than parkland, these were surrounded by increasingly elaborate gardens with formal terraces and fountains and urns, with broad gravel walks where you might stroll without getting your feet wet and flower beds brightly replanted two or three times a year. Beyond, in the pleasure ground, might be rockeries and rose gardens, dells of Himalayan rhododendrons and all manner of exciting new conifers, for this was the age of the plant hunter, when splendid new specimens came flooding into Britain from the farthest reaches of the globe. In addition, a walled kitchen garden, with glasshouses displaying the latest (and newly affordable) technology in heating, wrought iron and glass manufacture kept the household liberally supplied.

In their comprehensive study of the Victorian garden,[7] Joan Morgan and Alison Richards argue that the Victorian country house developed a particular role in maintaining the functions of society: that the country estate, and the house party culture it supported, became the primary means of putting one's economic, social and aesthetic credentials on display.[8] Absolutely crucial to this display were the skills of the head gardener. It was no longer sufficient simply to feed the family: he must dazzle all comers with his fabulous array of fruit and vegetables, thumbing his nose at the seasons to offer tender green beans in February, strawberries and cherries for Christmas dinner. Fruit had particular cachet, especially fruit grown under glass such as grapes and pineapples: the climax of the meal was the 'dessert' – not a pudding, but a spectacular display of fruit, as artfully arranged as a Dutch Old Master painting. The range of produce was phenomenal – in fruit alone there were 1,400 different sorts of apples, 140 varieties of peaches and nectarines, at least seven types of apricot, about a hundred kinds of plums and over forty varieties of cherry.[9] Indeed kitchen garden historian Susan Campbell confidently asserts that by the time of Queen Victoria's death in 1901, every esculent plant that could be grown in an English kitchen garden was to be found there.[10]

As well as food, the head gardener's glasshouses must provide pot plants and cut flowers to decorate the house, and showy exotics to stock the conservatories that were de rigueur from the 1850s onwards. Once the Prince Regent had made it fashionable to dine *à la Russe*, enjoying courses one at a time rather than all at once, elaborate table displays became the norm, and it was the head gardener's job to create them. Flowers were also required for personal adornment – ladies wore blooms in their hair, on their shoulders, at the waist and completed the ensemble with a bouquet. (A spray of eucharis on a stick was a particular favourite.) In houses of fashion, posies for the ladies and buttonholes for the gentlemen would be placed before each guest sitting down to dine.[11]

7 Joan Morgan and Alison Richards, *A Paradise out of a Common Field: The Pleasures and Plenty of the Victorian Garden*, Harper & Row, 1990.
8 Ibid, 22.
9 Eleanour Sinclair Rohde, *The Story of the Garden*, Hale, Cushman & Flint, 1932, republished by the Medici Society, 1989, 216.
10 Susan Campbell, *A History of Kitchen Gardening*, Frances Lincoln, 2005, 117.
11 Morgan and Richards, *A Paradise out of a Common Field*, 65–6.

Often the head gardener would have not one, but several houses to furnish with produce. He must manage a large staff, and keep au fait with new plants and new technologies. He must know how to grow every fashionable plant from pines to ferns to orchids (there were crazes for all of these). And he must keep everything in the highest state of polish, creating the illusion of a garden invulnerable to weather, weed or pest. So whether he was consolidating the social standing of an established family or demonstrating the acceptability of a new one, no one was more important to his employer's social credibility than the head gardener.

Some of these duties have changed little. Some have vanished without trace. The cultivation of pineapples, for example, no longer figures large in the modern head gardener's plan of work. Nor is he or she often called on, as Victorian garden guru John Claudius Loudon advises, to sprinkle paths with rosewater when an important party is expected, or to add 'a Poetical and Pastoral Air to the scene' by the judicious placing of comely livestock or by engaging 'a person with a flute'.[12] But the head gardener is still required to be master of a dauntingly vast array of skills, though now with many fewer hands at his or her disposal, and usually with only a fraction of the resources. The contemporary gardener is also likely to have a much more ambitious remit, too – seeking to please not just a privileged family, but a much wider and endlessly demanding public.

In fact it's hard to think of another job, except possibly being a vicar, which requires so wide-ranging and diverse a set of skills. Head gardeners must know how to care for trees in all their variety — as specimens, avenues, shelter belts, orchards or woodlands — as well as for shrubs, herbaceous plants, herbs, fruit and vegetables, and all plants growing under glass. They must maintain, and frequently design and construct, all the structures in the garden — walls, steps, terraces and paths, water features, pergolas, and all manner of garden buildings (or at least know the technical standards to which contractors must work). They must know how to use and maintain substantial and costly machinery. Then there's all the organization — managing and training staff, devising work schedules, budgets and management plans (sometimes for immensely costly restoration or development projects), grappling with health and safety,

Waste from the kitchen garden is gathered up for compost-making at West Dean.

---

12   J. C. Loudon, *An Encyclopædia of Gardening*, Longman, Hurst, Rees, Orme, and Brown, 1822, part 4, book 1, chapter 2: 'Of the Different Kinds of Garden in Britain', section 2105.

and the ticklish business of making the best use of volunteers. A lot of the larger gardens now depend on voluntary labour, and many head gardeners embrace the community aspects of volunteering, welcoming young offenders, people with mental health problems and all manner of disadvantaged groups into their gardens. (Others, however, mutter darkly that they didn't study horticulture in order to do social work.) Yet more diplomacy is required in managing the sometimes unrealistic expectations of employers, whether that be fending off multiple domestic roles (driver/handyman/security guard), opening seven days a week or holding large-scale events, any extra revenue from which must be weighed against the inevitable damage to the garden. And let's not forget the unpredictable effects of climate change, nor a tsunami of new plant diseases from *Chalara fraxinea* (ash dieback) and *Phytophthora ramorum* (sudden oak death) to box blight. All of this is just the daily load, before gardeners can embark on any kind of creative input – assuming they've done the guided tours, made sure no one gets locked in the car park and kept the garden safe from vandals and thieves.

It's a wonder any of them find time to pick up a trowel. In the heritage sector in particular, head gardeners are routinely required to produce interpretation materials, to devise amusements for children and to chat pleasantly to visitors. Many hours a week can be spent blogging. Or they're simply bogged down with admin: nearly all the gardeners interviewed complained they spent too much time at the computer, and considered it a waste of their time and skills. 'The job has become more demanding,' says Mike Calnan, Head of Gardens at the National Trust. 'We want to see a top quality garden, but there's still all this other stuff to be done. When you get on a plane there are two pilots. Maybe, in a big, complex garden, you need to have two people sharing the work.'

Calnan is well aware of the extraordinarily diverse skills held by the Trust's head gardeners. 'We have gardeners who are superlative plantspeople, such as Troy Scott Smith at Sissinghurst, or artists, like Mick Evans at Packwood House, or great ambassadors, mediators and trainers,' he says. 'Working on gardens spanning five hundred years of history, we have people who have blossomed into experts on early formal gardens or eighteenth-century shrubberies or Arts and Crafts gardens and everything in between. Academic research can only take us so far: it's the people on the ground who interpret and implement what history tells us, who know how planting from different periods really works, or what works in the space and what doesn't. It is they who bring history alive through their intervention and present it to the public as a living part of our cultural heritage.'

That cultural heritage has become big business: UK gardens attract some thirty-three million visitors a year,[13] of whom over a third come from abroad. We know too that horticulture in its various guises pumps some £9 billion into the UK economy each year, and provides employment for some three hundred thousand people.[14] As for the National Trust, former chairman Simon Jenkins believes that the charity's gardens are its most popular feature, and that 60 per cent of members join up first and foremost to enjoy the gardens.[15] Certainly, among its most visited pay-for-entry attractions, eight out of the top ten are gardens or houses with gardens.[16]

Gardens, then, must be regarded as economically significant. Equally, while no cost–benefit analysis has yet been devised to measure it, we can all recognize how powerfully gardens enhance the health and well-being of those who visit them, contributing to a broad spectrum of agendas from promoting physical and mental health, community engagement and social inclusion to teaching children basic maths and science and nurturing biodiversity. Above all, gardens are invaluable habitats for people: public gardens, suggests Calnan, have become substitutes for local parks — where people would once walk twenty or thirty minutes to the park to enjoy fresh air, family time and horticultural spectacle, now they'll drive to a garden. So however you look at it, few would dispute that being a head gardener is a thoroughly worthwhile and a hugely responsible job.

⸺•⸺

When J. C. Loudon compiled his great *Encyclopædia of Gardening* in 1822, he identified ten categories of 'Operators and Serving Gardeners', ranging from humble labourers to 'the summum bonum of garden servitude', the royal or court gardener. Though not at the very top of the tree (outranked by plant collectors and the keepers of botanic gardens), the head gardener, particularly of a 'mansion house', enjoyed considerable status. 'A gardener who undertakes such a situation', he wrote, 'should be at the head of his profession when he enters on it; and keep himself at the head of it, by taking care to be informed of every improvement and invention in his line, as they are discovered and made public. He must not only know all that is in books, but must be in advance in knowledge.'

13 *Horticulture Matters*, a report by partners in the horticulture industry, May 2013.
14 Ibid.
15 *Horticulture Week*, 5 July 2013.
16 National Trust Annual Report, 2014–15.

Loudon's choice of words is significant: in his mind there was no doubt that gardening was a profession. The skill and application required was clearly considerable, and the training long and demanding, covering not only plants, tools and pests and diseases, but meteorology, maths, surveying, 'the study of landscape gardening', 'systematic and physiological botany' and 'vegetable chemistry and geology'. A gardener must in addition make time for regular garden visiting, studying 'all the principal gardens for forty or fifty miles round', no doubt in a spirit of healthy competition.

In return for his endeavours, he might expect an ample staff, a pony and trap, a house-cow, free fuel, and 'a respectable house, near the kitchen garden, with a stable and a cow-house not far distant'.

His salary, however, was pitiful. Even when the estate garden was at its zenith, the average pay among the Gardeners of the Golden Afternoon was no more than a guinea a week. Alice Martineau, writing in 1913, protests: 'Gardeners' wages are on the whole very inadequate. Much is expected of them; not only hard and constant work in all weathers, but knowledge and artistic feeling and taste.' A head gardener, she observes, despite his 'long and arduous training from boyhood', is paid far less than the chauffeur. (These days the gardener is all too often the chauffeur as well.) It is a wonder 'that these able, intelligent men can be found for a payment so out of all proportion to their ability'.[17]

A century on, the situation has not changed one jot. If anything, it is worse. Gardening is no longer considered a profession, but a trade. Despite the existence of bodies such as the Professional Gardeners' Guild and the Institute of Horticulture, and despite the manifold skills of the head gardeners themselves, they remain little celebrated and appallingly paid. In addition, the chief perk of the job appears to have vanished: few employers now offer the accommodation that was once routinely provided. While no doubt it makes eminent sense to the business managers of the National Trust to convert their peripheral dwellings into chi-chi holiday cottages, it's a conundrum for the garden team. For who can afford to live in south-east England – or, indeed, many other parts of the country – on a gardener's wages?

'My career choices wouldn't be possible today,' says Michael Walker, Head Gardener at Trentham Gardens in Staffordshire. 'I was able to move around as I wished, because accommodation came with the job. People who might have been attracted to the job, living in a lovely house in a lovely place even where the salary is not too generous, now can't afford to do that.'

---

17 Alice Martineau, *The Herbaceous Garden*, 1913, quoted by Hoyles, *Bread and Roses*, 126–7.

Of course, it's not all about money. Every gardener interviewed here insists this career is a lifestyle choice: it's all about living surrounded by beauty, and making things more beautiful. It's about being creative and responsive, and in touch with nature. Martin Ogle, Head Gardener at Lowther Castle, speaks for them all: 'It's about being happy in what you're doing – even in the rain, even in the snow. Because where would you sooner be when the sun comes out again? It's not just a job – you've got to have a love for it. But you'll never tire of it, because every single day is different. You'll never be a rich man being a gardener, but you'll definitely be a very, very happy man.'

That's all well and good, but no one can feed a family on fresh air. Loudon was tireless in calling for better wages for gardeners, declaring that unless they were properly rewarded, there would soon not be enough of them to go round. It didn't happen in his day, but it appears to be happening in ours. There is now an acute skills shortage: a recent report by the horticultural industries found that 72 per cent of businesses are unable to find the skilled workers

The rigorous standards demanded of nineteenth-century gardeners are still upheld at West Dean – a place for everything and everything in its place.

they need.[18] Major employers such as English Heritage and the National Trust are struggling to find head gardeners of the right calibre. And even the best of them, suggests Troy Scott Smith, have an uncomfortable feeling that they are in some way lacking. 'I go to a lot of gardens that I used to visit ten or twenty years ago,' says Troy, 'and I don't think they are as good as they were. I think generally the standard of presentation, of plant interest, has declined. I don't feel that there's the depth of knowledge that the old head gardeners had. Things aren't being passed down as they used to be.'

Troy Scott Smith studying computer-generated drawings of Sissinghurst — part of acquiring the depth of knowledge he feels all head gardeners should aspire to.

Troy worries where the next generation is coming from. Back in Loudon's day, there was a recognized training route. A gardener started as an apprentice (often paying through the nose for the privilege), and after three years became a journeyman, moving from garden to garden to widen his experience, until at about the age of twenty-five he might become a foreman, taking charge of a section of a large garden, or a master gardener, taking sole charge of a smaller garden. From here he could progress, in time, to the dizzy heights of head gardener. The early years were hard: living conditions were often terrible and the system could be exploitative, but there was at least a clear career path, which remained in place until the Second World War.

But by the 1950s that way of life was over: by 1955, the gracious country houses where head gardeners had honed their skills were being demolished at a rate of one every five days. The expansion of the suburbs meant gardening became the province of amateurs — something which anyone could have a go at in their back gardens after Sunday lunch. It was left to the municipal parks departments to turn out skilled horticulturists, which they continued to do for another thirty years, until compulsory competitive tendering laid waste our public parks. That's how Alan Titchmarsh learned his trade, and the incomparable Roy Lancaster. When John Watkins, now Head of Landscape and Gardens at English Heritage, was an eighteen-year-old apprentice on day release, 75 per cent of his fellow students came from local authority

---

18 *Horticulture Matters*, 2013.

parks. Today the management of parks is almost universally contracted out, largely to an unskilled, strimmer-toting workforce. At the same time there has been a major decline in the number of horticultural courses run by the UK's higher education institutions, and a concomitant dearth of meaningful apprenticeships. The few opportunities that are offered find it hard to attract takers: when Martin Ogle offered an apprenticeship at Lowther Castle, there were only three applications. But then, as he points out, 'What nineteen year old would want to work in the rain for £2.65 an hour?'[19]

Partly to blame, suggests Mike Calnan, is the absurdly reductionist view we have of gardening – a view perpetuated by a largely unimaginative garden media that reduces gardening to 'What To Do When' or 'Hints and Tips', as if it were some form of outdoor housework. 'What is not factored in is the skill required to deal with a complex, ever-changing, living thing – planning way ahead … empathy … plant knowledge. Rather than taking account of their technical and artistic skills, employers tend to lump gardeners together as maintenance staff, a bit like janitors, whereas they need to be equated to quite different areas of activity.'[20]

A survey commissioned by the horticultural industry in 2013 echoes his opinion, finding that 70 per cent of eighteen year olds believe horticultural careers should only be considered by people who have 'failed academically', and nearly 50 per cent of under-twenty-fives think of horticulture as an unskilled job.[21]

This enrages Jim Buckland, the much-lauded head gardener at West Dean Gardens in Sussex. 'Gardening is not a career for dimwits,' he insists. Horticulture, however, is not an option that features large in the minds of most sixteen year olds – or their teachers. Even his own passion for growing was inspired not by gardens but a hippyish desire for a self-sufficient lifestyle. Trying to attract young people, he feels, is a bit of a red herring: better by far to concentrate on the career changers, who are already convinced of the value of gardening.

Over recent years, a succession of industry-wide initiatives has sought to recalibrate perceptions of the profession, each announced with much fanfare

---

19 It appears that rates of pay for both apprentices and experienced horticultural workers continue to be pegged to the agricultural minimum wage specified for land workers, rather than rising in response to the scarcity of skilled staff.
20 Writing in *The Practical Kitchen Gardiner* in 1727, Stephen Switzer felt much the same: 'I can't help considering a good Gardiner both as a philosopher and a politician, and one whose employ ought to place him very near the eye and favour of his master, and above that ill usage with which they commonly meet.' Quoted by Hoyles, *Bread and Roses*, 115.
21 *Horticulture Matters*, 2013.

but bringing little real progress. Meanwhile the National Trust, which employs some ninety head gardeners, has decided that the only way forward is to 'grow their own' and, working alongside English Heritage, has instituted a radical new training structure which aims to attract both school leavers and more mature candidates, and to raise standards at every level by offering working gardeners wider opportunities and continuing professional education. The aim is to equip promising gardeners with the variety of experience they need to reach the highest rung. We can only hope that pay scales will follow suit.

Of course, the Young Turks who train at Great Dixter, or RHS Wisley, Kew or the Royal Botanic Garden Edinburgh, bear the imprimatur of these establishments, and are soon snapped up by knowledgeable employers. But in the world at large, no distinction is made between the white van gardener who makes a living cutting lawns and trimming hedges, and those who are making finely judged decisions in historically significant landscapes on a daily basis. Dominic Cole, president of the Gardens Trust (the 2015 successor to the Garden History Society), has long argued that these head gardeners should enjoy the same professional status as the landscape architects and garden historians with whom they work. Some have exceptional expertise in plant science or specialist techniques — the kind of know-how that, say, in engineering would command universal esteem. Yet head gardeners persist in the public imagination as mere servants, almost comical figures — elderly, uneducated and unremittingly grumpy.

Maybe it is time to change the language, to refer to these highly skilled people as 'garden curators', a term commonly used in botanic gardens, and occasionally by those in charge of exceptional plant collections, such as Stephen Griffith at Abbotsbury Subtropical Gardens. They are, after all, curating horticultural heritage in a way directly analogous to the curator of any art collection or museum. We think of a museum curator with the utmost respect, as a person of learning. Why should it be different for head gardeners?

Indeed, it could be argued that they do all that their curatorial brethren do, and much more besides. For in addition to their technical, managerial and creative achievements, head gardeners have another, deeply significant role: in a world that has largely lost touch with weather and seasons, with the cycles of nature, they, like no one else, quietly reconnect us to the planet. Yes, they can put on a show, they can dazzle and amaze us with garden theatre. But more important, more lasting, more profound is the way they reignite our sense of beauty and belonging, reminding us of the everyday wonder of the natural world.

Gardens give us perspective in space and time.

In a historic garden today, a gardener has planted a young cedar, propagated from a tree brought from the Lebanon in the early eighteenth century. As the battered parent tree gradually fades and drops its weary limbs, so the young one grows to glory. The gardener will never see it. Yet, muses Mike Calnan, 'In how many jobs in this world do you have the opportunity to leave something that will last for hundreds of years? I can't think of many. Maybe if you're a great artist, perhaps …? But in a way that's what head gardeners are. The canvas is a bit bigger, that's all.'

The Gardener's Assistant, *which modestly claims to be 'a practical and scientific exposition of the art of gardening in all its branches', is still on the shelves at West Dean. This is the 1925 edition by William Watson; the first edition — by Robert Thompson, a noted expert on fruit at the RHS garden at Chiswick — was published in 1851.*

THE NATURALIST

NED PRICE
The Weir, Herefordshire

'It's all a matter of gently, gently . . .
in tune with the plants and the seasons.'

NED PRICE can't pin down his single happiest memory. It's a continuum of sunlight on water and rippling shadows, the azure flash of a kingfisher, the wind sighing through the willows. But maybe it's the day when, soon after arriving at The Weir, the National Trust garden on the banks of the Wye near Hereford, he took his young family down to the fishing jetty. Lying on the warm boards in the evening sunlight, they watched the sky dancing with sand martins, swallows and swifts, whirling in a feeding frenzy over the river, skimming so close they could almost reach out and touch them. And as the shadows lengthened, little by little, the birds faded away to be replaced by bats – Daubenton's bats gliding low over the water, pipistrelles darting above them, noctules riding high and straight as arrows through the sky. 'It was the night shift taking over from the day shift,' recalls Ned, his voice still full of wonder. 'It shows you how life is following its own rhythm all around you, even when you don't look to see it.'

Then there's the morning he saw an otter creeping out of the boathouse – only his second sighting in twenty-six years. When the river floods and the banks are submerged, all kinds of creatures take refuge in the building – stoats and weasels, hedgehogs, voles, even moles – though he has never worked out how they get in.

For Ned, gardening is all about wildlife, all about nature. There's nothing cosy in that relationship. The river that is the lifeblood of the garden is both its glory and its terror. It floods two or three times a year – the level can rise up to eighteen feet. Then visitors come out to watch it in spate, holding their breath at the foaming water and tree trunks hurtling down the valley. That used to be a winter drama.

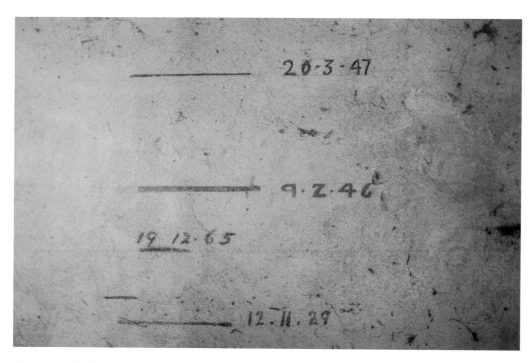

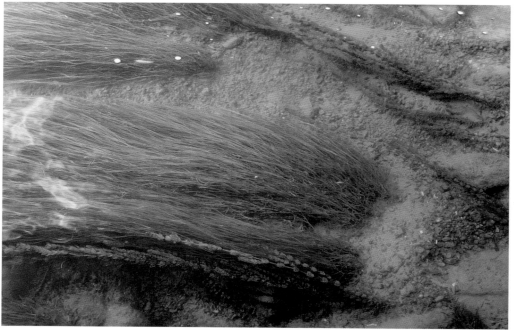

Now, more and more, it happens in summer too, scouring out the long tresses of water crowfoot that feed the jewelled clouds of damselflies.

Twice, during Ned's tenure, the river has frozen. Those winter nights, he would lie in bed and hear the eerie groan and crack of the ice. There are two old boys he chats to in the pub who remember the winter of 1947 — they swear there were ice floes floating past the garden, bearing cargoes of sheep.

It is that fickle, ever-changing river that defines the garden's spirit of place. The National Trust is big on Spirit of Place these days. It's a key thing in its management plans. But how do you put on a spreadsheet that vivid interaction of water and light; the hum of insects in the long grass; the sweet, wild pulse of the garden?

It's what brings the visitors here, that profound sense of connection to nature, Ned is sure of it. People have felt it for millennia. Down by the boathouse lies the remains of a Roman nymphaeum — a shrine devoted to the water nymphs who sported in the Wye. And it's what keeps Ned here, despite the gruelling working days spent crawling up steep banks and teetering on cliff edges, working patiently by hand. The garden is too steep for much in the way of machinery, and because he manages it organically, there's no resort to labour-saving chemicals.

Of the garden's ten acres, five extend along a narrow, precipitous slope overhanging the riverbank, divided by twisting stairways and meandering paths. It is essentially a creation of the 1920s, when Roger Parr, a successful Manchester banker with a fancy for fishing, bought The Weir as a country retreat. It was Parr, or rather his head gardener, William Boulter, who secured the riverbank with heavyweight concrete defences, who planted the topiary mounds that characterize the central parts of the garden, laid out staircases snaking down the slope, and a long walk along the top. It was Parr's financial muscle that hoisted in mighty stones from Cheddar Gorge to create a rockery, and flung a bridge across the narrow gully at the highest point of the garden. From here there are magnificent views downstream towards Hereford, and back across ancient water meadows towards the Brecon Beacons and the louring cloudscapes of Wales.

Over the years, Ned has gently loosened Parr's authoritarian grip on the landscape, blurring the formal central part with a succession of wild flowers, opening up the flatter woodland walk to the west, encouraging spring bulbs to intermingle more naturally on the grassy banks to the east. Spring comes early to these south-facing banks, carpeting them with snowdrops, primroses and violets, bright blue puddles

PAGES 28–29 *The ever-shifting moods of the river define the spirit of the garden.*
OPPOSITE, ABOVE *High on the walls of the boathouse are recorded the water levels reached in previous floods.*
OPPOSITE, BELOW *The long trails of water crowfoot in the river will later be spangled with tiny white buttercup flowers.*

of glory of the snow. Then as they begin to fade, there's a second flush of blue from Ned's favourite, *Scilla messeniaca*, then cyclamen and ipheion, camassia and spring snowflakes (*Leucojum vernum*), and everywhere clumps of narcissi, from the first spirit-lifting sightings of *N.* 'February Gold' and *N.* 'March Sunshine', tousled sheets of wild *N. pseudonarcissus*, through to the late old variety *N. poeticus* with its burning centre and delicate scent — so much more graceful than the modern pheasant's eye varieties.

Gardening here is all about the art that conceals art — not too tidy, and richly atmospheric. It is not always appreciated. Ned remembers two disconsolate matrons making their way back to the car park. 'Excuse me,' said one, 'we can't seem to find the garden . . .'

'That holistic approach is what is important to me — and the worst thing for that is when people want everywhere tidy.'

———•———

There are people who take to the soil when still in nappies. Ned wasn't one of them. His father was in the army, and they moved every three years — never anywhere long enough to make a garden. By the time he was sixteen years old, Ned had lived in Germany and Belgium, Cyprus, Egypt and Wales.

As a teenager in Colwyn Bay on the chilly north Welsh coast, he was driven out of bed on Saturday mornings to mow the lawn — enough, he thinks now, to put anyone off gardening. But he was always interested in wildlife.

'As a ten year old', he recalls, 'I had bug books and butterfly books and a microscope. Then, as a teenager, I spent a lot of my time wandering the hills and the woods with friends. I'd go off exploring and find birds' nests and watch foxes. Being outside was the important thing, being close to nature, seeing animals, trees and plants.'

There's a memory of the keen young naturalist that haunts him still. When he was ten, in Belgium, he spotted, for the first and only time in his life, a swallowtail butterfly. 'I was so excited when I caught it that I took it to show to a neighbour, who was a keen butterfly man. Together we killed it and pinned it to a board. And I've never seen another one since, except on the television. A nice example of conservation!' Even after all these years, Ned looks as if he could cry. 'These days, thankfully, when you see something interesting you take a picture.' Ned has become an avid fan of digital photography, and spends long hours on the Internet, researching his finds.

The Weir is best known for its spring flowers — huge carpets of small bulbs naturalized down the banks and under the trees, giving a continuous display from early January well into May. Ned is gratified when visitors think the show is all wild.

His first jobs as a teenager were summer gardening jobs for the local council — he would always rather be outside than in. But there was no thought then of gardening as a career. Instead, he grew his hair and set off on the hippy trail, overland to India and back again. He would take any job that earned money, labouring, or working in factories, then be off again, to Holland or Germany, Greece or Afghanistan, for three, six, nine months at a time. 'Looking back, I saw amazing things: valleys ablaze with rhododendrons in Nepal; cloud forest trees dripping with orchids, but that was before I was really interested. I wish I could do it now: I'd get so much more out of it.'

'That's the beauty of gardening, that every day there's something new. You're like a little child in a toy shop — there's always something happening, whether it's the birds, the butterflies, the insects or the plants.'

In his late twenties, now married with a baby, he got his first permanent gardening job, with cottage, on a private estate. Then the owner sold up, leaving him homeless. Ned hastily took a factory job in mid-Wales, close to his wife's family. Which is how he came, one Sunday afternoon, to be taking tea with his in-laws at Powis Castle, the most ravishing, most theatrical and most horticulturally distinguished garden in Wales.

'We got chatting with a gardener, who mentioned they were about to launch a training programme. Though I had worked as a gardener, I had never had proper training: I would go home each night and get my books out and read up what I had to do the next day — how to prune a rose bed, or how to plant asparagus.' Ned looked around him. It certainly beat the production line. 'The idea of learning how to do things properly really appealed, so I signed up.'

Ned spent two years at college and two years at Powis working under Head Gardener Jimmy Hancock — horticultural adventurer, bold experimenter with half-hardy plants and originator of the invaluable *Artemisia* 'Powis Castle'. 'Jimmy was a great gardener and a great plantsman — and I liked his approach to it all. He showed me that a lot of gardening is trial and error, that you need to have the confidence to try new things. But first you need the background information to make it a reasonable bet. He was in charge — but he would give you ideas, guide you. He taught by example. It was he who encouraged me to look for a job with the National Trust.'

Presently, one came up at The Weir, a little known garden remarkable for its spring bulbs, but very much in need of some TLC. 'I drove over to look at it and when I got back, Jimmy said, "What's the garden like?" And I said, "There isn't one."' But it's a beautiful place, and that's what drew me in — the river, the woods, the wildlife . . . And I loved the idea of being the first gardener in charge here.

The mood of the garden changes hour by hour with the light on the river.

'I was excited by the challenge – it was totally overgrown. When I walked around with my son, who was two, I had to put him on my shoulders because the nettles and brambles and thistles over the paths were taller than he was.'

In those days the garden opened only in the spring, just three days a week. Visitors were few, leaving their pennies in an honesty box. Ned found himself with a staff of two who departed each day at lunchtime, and very much left to his own devices.

'It was up to me to do what I wanted after the bulbs had flowered. And that's how we started leaving them to seed and spread,' he says. 'Soon you start to notice the wild flowers coming up, so you extend the season a bit more, and then you start to see butterflies and moths feeding on the flowers, so you leave them as long as possible, and then come the birds and the mice feeding on the seed, so you leave it a bit longer – until you get to where we are now, where we are reluctant to cut at all, because as soon as we do, we're removing habitat or food.'

These days, Ned leaves the garden standing till late August – then it's flat out till Christmas, clipping the hedges and clearing the banks, while still carefully maintaining a food supply and pockets of habitat for the wildlife.

As a result, the garden is full of birds — nearly forty different kinds at the last count — attracted by the abundant insect life, including rarities like the hummingbird hawkmoth and club-tailed dragonfly. Meanwhile the flora steadily becomes more species-rich: 'In one square yard I can show you buttercups, campanulas, brunnera, primula, violets, dog's mercury, mousetails and various umbellifers.' Rare ferns have popped up in the rockery, and cowslips and twayblades: the wild yellow orchid *Neottia* (formerly *Listera*) *ovata* now flourishes in the grass.

There are still a few visitors who complain about the messiness, especially in July and August, but as wildlife gardening has become more popular, public understanding has gradually caught up. Chelsea, these last few years, has been awash with nettles and dandelions, and even the RHS has finally cottoned on to the importance of pollinators. It's not in Ned's nature to be smug, but he cannot help a wry smile as the cause he has been espousing for twenty-five years suddenly becomes horticultural high fashion.

'I have to be glad that people are finally coming round to that way of thinking, and adopting a more holistic viewpoint. It's not just about growing flowers any more, but seeing that birdlife, mammals and insects are all part and parcel of our gardens, though we ignore them most of the time. I'd make it even wilder if I could.'

In 2009, however, Ned embarked on a project that would satisfy the most fastidious gardener — the restoration of the estate's walled kitchen garden. In just four years, with the help of a loyal band of volunteers, this derelict two acre site, with broken greenhouses and tumbledown walls, has been transformed into a pristine potager. It's a colossal commitment of time and effort, for which Ned received just one extra gardener for just one season and a princely seed budget of £100. The Trust is delighted with it of course — it brings in summer visitors. (Visitors have gone up from four thousand to twenty-four thousand on Ned's watch.) And Ned is immensely proud of what has been achieved here. But he can't help looking enviously over his shoulder at large gardens like Hidcote — well resourced and financially secure. 'The trouble is that people expect that standard of gardening across the Trust — but Hidcote has one acre per gardener and we have five.' Often, it feels like running to stand still.

———◆———

The question must be asked, then, why Ned has not chosen to move on. To get on in gardening, you have to keep moving around. 'There are things more important than money,' says Ned quietly. 'It all comes down to family in the end — because I moved every three years, I wanted to give my children a more stable background. And also, it's such a beautiful place to live. I'm in a fortunate position — I get the house with the job. I've lived on private estates in a similar position, but here there's no

The walled kitchen garden has been restored on a shoestring, and has proved popular with visitors and volunteers alike. Ned sees it as a welcome counterbalance to The Weir's more naturalistic attractions.

owner to bump into. Here, I can go out at night and watch the sunset, and I have the place to myself. There's a quality of life here that is higher than I could get anywhere else.

'Living on the property you become a part of it, in a way that you don't if you're just coming in to work each day. Living in a place – it gets in the DNA.' There's a downside, of course – the total absence of nine to five. He's out there at night, closing down the greenhouse, and again on Saturdays and Sundays. Holidays just don't seem to happen: the erstwhile world traveller has left the country for one single week in the last twenty years. (You can't help thinking that the National Trust is making a mistake, getting rid of tied cottages for gardeners in favour of holiday lets. How do you value such a profound sense of ownership?)

Ned won't move on now: despite his youthful looks, he is sixty and approaching retirement. Not that he wants to retire – he'd gladly stay on another decade.

There are worse ways to spend a life, he reflects. 'I've been here long enough to observe what effect we have had on the garden. Not many people have that kind of job satisfaction. When you turn on the television, you hear all about things becoming extinct – plants, animals, birds. But since I've come to The Weir, everything's coming back; we have otters we didn't use to have; ravens we didn't use to have; buzzards and red kites; we're seeing birds and butterflies I haven't seen before. It's good to know it's not all bad news.'

THE GENEROUS
GARDENER

FERGUS GARRETT
Great Dixter, East Sussex

'Be generous in the way that you garden,
and in the way that you share it with other people.'

CLIMBING UP TO the gallery in the 500-year-old Great Barn at Great Dixter, head gardener Fergus Garrett catches his hand on a rough piece of timber. A bright bead of blood forms on his finger. There is a rare moment of stillness in the half dark, as he licks the blood away. The splinter doesn't budge. 'It's a good one,' he says approvingly. 'I'll leave that there for my girls. They'll like getting that one out.'

'Won't that hurt?'

'Yes,' he says, unruffled.

You might consider it an excess of love, to allow yourself to be gouged by two eager little girls with needles. But that is a condition of which Fergus is often accused, and in which he finds neither fear nor shame.

Above all things, Fergus loves his wife and family. He says he only studied horticulture so he could hang around at college to be near the lovely and unattainable Amanda Ferguson. Reader, he married her.

He loves Great Dixter, the East Sussex garden that has been his life since he was twenty-six years old – and not just the garden, but the woods, the fields, the ponds, the rickety half-timbered house and the jumble of farm buildings that make up the Dixter estate.

He loved his friend and employer Christopher Lloyd, the famously iconoclastic and irascible gardener-writer, with a complicated, profound, many-layered love

that blended filial piety, a quasi-parental protectiveness, admiration, respect and amused exasperation with the exhilarating bond of partners in crime, as together they shook the horticultural establishment to its roots.

Since Christo (as all his friends called him) died in 2006, that love has been channelled into keeping Great Dixter alive, not only in terms of borders or buildings, but in creating a Great Dixter family — a messy, unpredictable, dynamic, dysfunctional family encompassing misfits, obsessives, lost souls, saints and creative geniuses of every kind, united by their love for the place and their love and admiration for Fergus. It is they who give the garden its special spark, beyond the exuberant and innovative planting for which Great Dixter has become famous. There are the students who come from all over the world, desperate to hone their skills at what is essentially the premier horticultural finishing school in Europe. (Fergus chooses them carefully, balancing energy and drive with qualities of empathy and a willingness to muck in.) It is clear why he would employ the luminous Rachael Dodd, who radiates kindness and intelligence in equal measure, or Graham Hodgson, whom he describes as the most skilful practical gardener he has ever known. But why take a chance on the homeless teenager who's never done a hand's turn in his life? Or the lad who boldly asked for a break, while confessing he had been 'in and out of trouble with life'?

'I told him if he put a foot wrong, he'd be out, and he never did put a foot wrong while he was here,' says Fergus. 'He's now gone on to a responsible job elsewhere. The rest of us have families behind us; we have some kind of support. These kids have nothing, so you make allowances. You give them a bit more slack — not too much, because it's not fair on the others — but if that person wants to help themselves, we'll try to help them do that. But if ever I thought they were disrespectful or taking the mickey, I wouldn't give them the time of day.

'Of course it would be easier in some ways not to do this,' he continues. 'And if I felt the place was suffering I wouldn't, but as long as we can manage to work it, it makes all our lives more interesting. People are full of surprises.'

There are the dyslexics, written off as no-hopers at school, who have blossomed into starry gardeners themselves. At the other end of the scale is the Classics scholar from Oxford who found he preferred real shrubs and trees to the groves of Academe. There's Richard Asher, the ex-policeman, weary of uniformed life, who is now the estate woodsman, after money was raised to fund the post. There's Simon Johnson, who turns Richard's forest gatherings into benches and boxes and ladders, exhibiting a dexterity he never had when flipping pizzas. And there's

The ever-changing pot display round the porch has long been one of Great Dixter's most admired attractions.

Lewis Bosher, whose family moved around so much when he was young that he had little in the way of formal schooling, though his mother managed to home-educate him even in difficult circumstances. He came to the garden as a volunteer aged just fourteen, and Great Dixter paid for him to go through college. Now he's assistant head gardener and Fergus has high hopes that he will succeed him.

'He's turned out to be the most unusually creative guy I've had here for years,' enthuses Fergus. 'His brain works in a slightly different way — he does these very quirky things that are brilliant, things you wouldn't ever think of. His pot displays are inspired. He is also kind and generous to everyone.'

Helping Lewis today is his younger brother, Hayden, who, like so many youngsters in rural areas, is finding his job prospects limited. But watching him patiently barrowing soil and mixing compost, Fergus has already noted his conscientiousness and his carefulness, and resolved to try to do something for him. Even the garden cat was rescued from a bombsite in Kabul.

Why does he do it?

'Because I can,' he says softly. 'When I was young, I didn't have a family here. My mother, who is Turkish, had returned home and my father wasn't really involved, so the people who made all the difference to my life were the few who went out of their way to help, who were kind.

'So I like kind people. As you get older you realize it's the most important thing, and you hope you can set an example. I like being a giving person. I'm in a place of privilege where I can make things happen for people. As long as people work hard for you and really want to achieve something, you give them everything . . .'

The most beautiful thing that is cultivated at Dixter is generosity of spirit.

———◆———

Fergus would say that generosity is part and parcel of his Turkish heritage. He and his elder brother were brought up by his mother near Istanbul (she and his British father divorced when he was a baby), but the family moved to England when he was twelve to improve the boys' education. Fergus looks back on these times as monochrome interludes between his real life in Turkey: home was his grandmother's house, bursting with vegetables and flowers, to which they would return every holiday and resume their place in village life.

'We came from a very comfortable family background in Turkey. We lived in a poor village where we had this amazing house, and from an early age we were taught to share — money, toys, whatever we had. When I was fourteen or fifteen years old we would gather up the kids in the village and pay for them all to go to the cinema. My brother would be at the front of the row and I would be at the

Neil, the garden cat, is an Afghan refugee. Fergus's brother, who found her, named her after a colleague he worked with in Afghanistan.

back, and we'd march them all off to the pictures and march them back again. It was a family thing that went deep.'

When he was eighteen, his mother moved back permanently, leaving the boys to a rackety student life in Brighton. His brother (now a civil servant) was his mainstay then, and they remain close. From here, Fergus went on to Wye College in Kent to read agriculture, dreaming of becoming a farmer in Turkey. (He still says, if he were not a gardener, he can think of no better job than selling fat, glossy vegetables in a Turkish market.) The reality of intensive agriculture, however, proved less appealing, and it was no great struggle, prompted by a lovesick heart, to switch to horticulture. He found he liked it, and after a stint working for the Brighton parks department, returned to Wye to study for a BSc.

It was at this point that he got to know Christopher Lloyd, when he came for a weekend with fellow student Neil Ross, already a volunteer at Great Dixter. Lloyd loved to surround himself with people, especially the young, and his weekends were legendary — a heady whirl of champagne, whisky, inquisitorial garden walks and dodging the teeth of an imperious tribe of dachshunds. The two men hit it off, and maintained a lively correspondence as Fergus moved around from job to job. First he went to Stoneacre in Kent, the dreamily romantic garden made around a medieval hall house by Rosemary Alexander, founder of the English Gardening School.

'There are other gardens, like
Sissinghurst, which are equally
beautiful but slightly cold.
Dixter has a warmth, and
the warmth emanates from
Fergus, and from the crazy
people he gathers round him.'

LEWIS BOSHER,
ASSISTANT HEAD GARDENER

*The spirit of abundance reigns supreme at
Great Dixter.*

She had him marked down for great things from the first: 'He never went anywhere', she recalls, 'but at a run.' Then, on the advice of Lloyd, he spent some months with Beth Chatto, who remains an inspiration in his life. (No one, he believes, can match Beth's delicacy of observation.) A stint with the Sackler family followed, in Switzerland and the South of France. It was a planting of dazzling orange gazanias with magenta mesembryanthemums under the blue skies of Cap d'Antibes that he believes prompted Lloyd to invite him to Great Dixter. At first he declined, fearful it would ruin their friendship. But Lloyd wouldn't take no for an answer. And so began an endlessly stimulating, testing, occasionally argumentative, non-stop, gleeful conversation about plants that was to last for the next fifteen years.

'That man — gardening's his heartbeat.'
MICK EVANS

By the time Fergus arrived Lloyd was seventy-one and had been gardening at Great Dixter all his life. He had been born in the house — a glorious mishmash of largely medieval fragments cobbled together in 1910 by Christo's father, Nathaniel, with the help of Sir Edwin Lutyens. The garden, laid out at this time, remained largely unaltered, a classic Arts and Crafts framework of brick and yew enclosures, within which the ceaselessly questing and adventurous Lloyd could indulge his fascination with plants.

Some of his early gusto, however, had gone, along with elasticity of back and limb, and the garden was at a low ebb. 'When I came here Christo was struggling to keep on top of everything,' recalls Fergus. But by relieving him of the headache of day-to-day management, specifically people management, he was able to rekindle Lloyd's joy in the garden. 'He wanted to have fun. He sought out character and individuality in plants as he did with people — he tried to get under their skin.' It was this quality that made Lloyd such a vivid writer and such an inventive gardener. Always contemptuous of the dead hand, as he saw it, of good taste, he revelled in bold colour and theatrical plant combinations at a time when ladylike pastels were all the mode, and was loud in defence of dayglo-leaved cannas and whopping orange dahlias. In fact the more generally reviled the plant, the better — he was even known to champion spotty laurel. But every single plant in the garden had to earn its keep: his standards were exacting, and mediocrity was no more to be endured in the flower bed than in the parlour. If Fergus, with all his vigour and enthusiasm, brought the garden a new vitality, Lloyd gave his young gardener an equally precious gift. He taught him to look, to look hard, with precision and without prejudice; to see the qualities inherent in every plant; to see the garden changing, ebbing and flowing, not just season by season but week by week, day by day.

'We had a common goal in what we wanted to make of the place, and he had confidence in me to do what was needed,' says Fergus. 'He felt he could mould me, and he did, in terms of sensibility and skill.' Together they developed a complex system of planting in layers to deliver surge after surge of continuous colour, so that the Long Border in particular became a thing of wonder, providing constant fireworks from April to October. They famously ripped out the formal rose garden, replacing it with an 'exotic' garden of outsize foliage, thus creating a trend for 'jungle' gardens that would endure for (so far) more than two decades. The lawns round the topiary grew long and shaggy. The Lutyens steps were ornamented with succulents. The pot displays around the porch grew ever more extravagant.

Fergus's great contribution was to introduce a certain looseness and flow — more self-seeders, more grasses, more link plants — with no loss of intensity, but somehow more room to breathe. Since Lloyd's death the garden has gone from strength to strength, the effects seeming ever more artless (in fact, nothing could be further from the truth) and the season ever longer. Even on a rainy November afternoon, Great Dixter throbs with vibrant life.

Fergus credits Christopher Lloyd with teaching him to look, to appreciate the unique character and potential of every plant — a skill that Fergus seeks to develop in his students.

A healthy reserve of plants lies waiting behind the scenes, to keep the borders fresh and dynamic.

'I do sometimes wonder what Christo would think,' muses Fergus. 'I know I'm using things he wouldn't have given houseroom, such as cow parsley. But he'd hate it if the garden became a museum piece, if we just let the dust settle on it.'

Just before he died, Lloyd told Fergus that the fifteen years he had spent with him at Great Dixter had been the happiest years of his life. 'That was the best present he could have given me,' says Fergus. 'And that, I would say, has been my greatest achievement, to take someone who could be a difficult character sometimes and to mould a team around him that he liked and trusted and could be easy with in the garden. We pulled the garden up one or two notches in places, but it was always a great garden. We had such good times – all the students sitting round in the Great Hall while he read them Saki stories – those images will be with them for the rest of their lives.'

Does he still miss him? 'Massively,' he replies with fervour. 'We didn't always agree on everything. He could be cantankerous and brash and slam his fist on the table and shout, "Damn you!", but he could always say sorry and so could I.

'I was in awe of his mind and creativity: he was so unusual in his ideas. And I came to love him as if he were family, and together that made such a strong bond.' It's hard to be the surviving half of so celebrated a double act: Bacall without Bogart, Gilbert without George . . . It's harder still to think of any great gardening duo that did not perish with the death of one partner. Joseph Paxton, outliving his employer the Duke of Devonshire, no longer had the need to get dirt under his fingernails, and became a tycoon. Lutyens, free of the tutelary spirit of Gertrude Jekyll, turned to building palaces. As first Vita Sackville-West and then her husband, Harold Nicolson, relinquished the reins on Sissinghurst, their place was taken by another formidable pair, Pamela Schwerdt and Sibylle Kreutzberger, and the garden acquired by the National Trust. (That was a fate that Lloyd had specifically ruled out, often saying he would rather Dixter withered and died with him.) 'But I don't feel like Morecambe without Wise,' says Fergus stoutly. 'I have lots of Wises here. Perry Rodriguez and Kathleen Leighton still work here and they had a long working relationship with Christo. There are trustees like Kemal Mehdi and Geoffrey Dyer who knew Christo well and who are close to the soul of Dixter; and old friends such as Anna Pavord, Colin Hamilton and Keith Sangster with whom I feel an intimacy in the garden, and it feels almost like Christo is present when they are here. Dan Pearson is someone I like seeing in the garden because he understands it at a level I enjoy and conversation with him is always deep. Tom Wright was both Christo's student and my teacher, and important to us both. No one can take Christo's place, but each one, in their own little way, makes up for his loss.'

—◆—

Clearly, it wasn't always sunshine working for Christopher Lloyd. But this is not to say that it is easy working for Fergus Garrett. (It must be even worse living with him – his idea of a perfect day is getting up at four in the morning and getting in a solid six hours' gardening before coming home for breakfast.)

He can be fiery, he confesses, and autocratic. While everyone is welcome to proffer an opinion, ultimately his word is law. 'It's frustrating if you've put a lot of work into something and he just doesn't like it,' says Education Officer Catherine Haydock, who has often been in this position. 'What's even more annoying is that when you go through it, he's almost always right.'

'Fergus is very exact,' says Graham. 'He knows he's a control freak. Everything has to be tickety-boo and he has to know exactly what's going on. If you make a mistake you'll know all about it – but it makes you a better worker.'

He has no patience with slackers; he loathes people who are selfish or bullying or greedy. As a result, there is much in this world that makes him very angry.

His way is not to grumble, but to do what he can to put things right. For example, his outrage that our finest nurserymen can barely scrape a living has led to Great Dixter holding two plant fairs a year, simply to offer them a platform. No one can buy their way in: attendance is by invitation only. These are not so much commercial events as something between a party and a symposium, where the chief objective is to get together and talk plants. Fergus invariably spends the mornings directing the traffic in the car park, then retreats to the kitchen to prepare moussaka for ninety. Later on, everyone sits round the bonfire till the wee small hours, chewing the fat in an excited babble of English, Dutch, German, French and horticultural Latin. 'It's like an informal convention,' he explains delightedly, 'our youngest students and our greatest plantsmen all sitting down together.'

'I hate people who are bullies and shits. And I'm happy when the good people in this trade win and are successful, because there are a lot of good people, and it's a tough industry to be in.'

It's also a lot of work; and if Fergus has a fatal flaw, it lies in taking on too much. It is not as if he were not already busy enough with gardening, training, workshops, symposia and the travails of running a small charity. Fergus also writes and lectures widely, serves as president of the Northiam Horticultural Society (Great Dixter's home village) and sits on various committees for the RHS. He knows he says yes to too many things; he knows he spreads himself too thin.

He'll drive to North Yorkshire and back in a day because there simply isn't time to stay overnight, and if dashing off to the States for an impromptu lecture tour will allow him to keep a promising trainee for longer, he'll do it.

Catherine has long given up trying to get him to adhere to standard practice. Placements are supposed to be for a year, but he'll keep students on till he considers them 'finished' and ready to move on. Work disputes are as often as not resolved with a wrestle on the lawn. 'There's definitely a Dixter way of doing things,' says Catherine with a smile, 'and you have to get that if you're going to work here.'

But name an ambitious young person in horticulture who *doesn't* want to work here . . . Even youngsters with very respectable jobs elsewhere, with Kew, or with the National Trust, will pitch up for volunteer working weekends, just to enjoy the vibe. That's how gardener Rachael Dodd first came to Great Dixter. 'The first thing that strikes you is how everybody involved is so excited about the plants and the garden,' she says. 'There's a lot of hope for gardening here, a lot of belief. It draws people to the place, but it also radiates something out. Working here, we rediscover the wonder of why we do what we do.'

'I don't know how many people get the chance to work and live that every day,' she continues. 'There are aspects of it in many places. There are other individuals who

Fergus, famously, takes life at a run.

have that curiosity and drive and that passion to share it with others. However, it's sort of *amplified* here. I have never seen any rival to Fergus's own personal commitment, how he strives to produce something wonderful in the truest sense, but never loses sight of people being the most important thing.'

It shows. One of the staff has come back to work straight from a family funeral. No one expected to see her for some days yet, but she'd rather be here, she says, where she feels supported and can soothe herself with quiet, repetitious work. Fergus folds her in his arms and she weeps for a while, soundlessly, on his shoulder. Then she wipes her eyes and disappears behind a hedge. Fergus signals to the others to let her go. It's part of what gardens are, to be healing.

Would he ever move on? It's something he's been asked many times, yet he pauses a while: it's an attractive quality, listening hard to what people say, then thinking before replying.

If Great Dixter changed, in its essence, he would. But the garden is now a charitable trust, run by a band of trustees as committed as he to preserving its unique quality, its integrity. 'I'm happy that though Christo has gone we haven't lost the name or the quality or the charm of the place,' he reflects. 'I'm happy that we don't let it out for weddings. I'm happy that we haven't turned the barn into a restaurant, but that someone's using it as a working environment, practising a skill that's being lost elsewhere. I could go off and make a garden in Istanbul, but my loyalty is to Christo, and it still feels like an adventure. If we did the same thing every year it wouldn't, but we don't: we have new students every year, we try new plants every year, so it's always exciting. And the bigger picture is the energy we put into the students, so this way of life spreads by a ripple effect. When they go on to other places they will make sure that our skills are passed on and that people are looked after.'

Even with massive support from the extended Dixter family, it's by no means easy. Like every small charity, they are perpetually in need of more money, having to scrimp and save. Just repairing the roof cost £70,000. However, at the time of writing, they have finally made it into the black, and visitor numbers are the highest ever. His long-term ambition is commendably simple: to pass Great Dixter on to the next generation in a manner of which Lloyd would have been proud.

But what of personal ambitions? 'I want to be excellent at what I do,' he says earnestly. A man who in 2015 received the Veitch Memorial medal (one of the RHS's highest honours) might think he'd consider he's made the grade. But no. 'I want to increase my knowledge and my growing ability: to be able to graft in four or five different ways, to grow all the seed I want to, and really know my subject inside out. I've made a name through all the lectures and the media, but that's nothing compared to the true skill of gardening.'

As head gardener at Great Dixter, he believes his role is equally to garden and to teach. The two are indivisible. What he teaches is not just how to garden, but how to nurture. 'The biggest lesson life has taught me is to love and be supportive. At the end of the day, it's not about material things, it's about people. You will succeed if you are good at your job, creative, hungry for information and eager to learn. But the message I want to pass on above all others is to be generous. Always be generous in the way that you garden, and in the way that you share it with other people.'

Fergus is committed to preserving the essential texture of Great Dixter — honouring the spirit of Christopher Lloyd without turning it into a shrine.

A SURVIVOR'S TALE

PAUL PULFORD
Roof Garden at Southbank Centre's
Queen Elizabeth Hall, London

*'Life goes in seven year cycles — seven years from building
a hostel garden with crackheads and junkies to this . . .'*

PAUL PULFORD, aka Scruffy (the moniker borrowed from his dog), just
can't keep still. He jigs around from foot to foot, scrabbles fruitlessly in his
pockets for cigarette papers, repeatedly scrapes the hair out of his eyes, leaving a
faint, earthy trail over his ravaged, once handsome face. All the time a torrent, a
cataract of words gushes from his lips — urgent, funny, impetuous, heartbreaking.
In four hours he does not once pause for breath.

Partly it's nervous energy, partly the irrepressible enthusiasm of a ten-year-
old boy, but chiefly it's the habitual jitteriness of the junkie, a restlessness that
can never be stilled. In a way, it's been the making of him. 'For seven years,' he
explains, 'I was on the street. I was a heroin addict, an alcoholic, I had mental
health problems. I didn't give a shit if I woke up the next morning, and I wasn't
going to survive another winter outdoors . . .'

It's a story he's told many times, to many people — celebrities from Foreign
Secretary Boris Johnson, actress Barbara Windsor, garden designer and TV
presenter Joe Swift and conservationist Bill Oddie (like Paul, a keen birder and
sufferer from bipolar disorder); to schoolchildren, delinquents, tweedy gentlefolk
from the RHS and, most importantly, to countless other dossers and crackheads.

Repetition hasn't made him glib. He tells his tale with ardent sincerity. Best
of all, it has a happy ending. For the former junkie is now head gardener of a
high profile garden, created on the south bank of the Thames on top of London's

Queen Elizabeth Hall. It is a haven of many kinds – for birds, bees, butterflies, wild flowers, harassed office workers and lost souls like himself. Over 150 different kinds of native British herbs and flowers bloom between orchard and ornamental trees in log-edged raised beds, where charms of goldfinches descend at dawn to feast on the teasels, and where nesting wrens thread the air with their improbably loud song. Exotic vegetables thrive in ranks of raised beds, where more wild flowers, seeded into paving cracks, are encouraged to remain as pollinators. Nectar-rich climbers twine over pergolas and spill over the once bleak concrete parapets, now busy with butterflies and bees. The harsh paving is blanketed with soft, daisy-spangled lawn, where workers and visitors kick off their shoes and picnic and sprawl in the sun.

This oasis has been created by Paul and his team of gardeners, once loosely known as 'Grounded and Scruffy', now rebranded 'Grounded Ecotherapy' and officially a social enterprise with responsibility for the maintenance of the garden. All are service users, formerly homeless, most wrestling with a drug or alcohol habit. Piquantly, the garden was recently voted one of the coolest places in London to stop for a drink.

———— ·•· ————

The average life expectancy for a homeless man in the UK is forty-two years. Paul was already forty-five when in around 2002 he was persuaded by outreach worker Penny Lancaster to move into an East London hostel – a first tentative step in turning his life around. He should remember, she urged him, who he was before life took a wrong turning, what made him happy as a child, what he wanted to be when he grew up.

'That bit was easy,' he says. 'I've always been interested in nature. When I grew up I wanted to be a nature warden on a reserve – I picked that up from watching BBC One's *Countryfile* on a Sunday, and it seemed like the best job in the world.'

Paul never knew his natural mother, a prostitute in the East End. But he counted himself lucky to have been adopted by a couple in Havant, near Portsmouth, the second of five adopted children. There was no money, but it was a happy childhood. They lived on a vast warren of a council estate, but on the very edge, so Paul had only to cross the road and he could be off in the woods and the fields, birds'-nesting, watching the butterflies and insects, building dens or camping with the Scouts. Paul's adoptive dad was confined to a wheelchair, disabled by polio and diabetes, so as far back as he can remember, Paul did the gardening: he claims

Paul boasts his rooftop garden has the best view in Britain, overlooking Big Ben and the London Eye.

Plants rich in nectar and seeds provide a valuable inner-city fuelling stop for birds and butterflies.

to have been shoving a petrol mower around from the age of six. At twelve he was given his first gardening book for Christmas – *The Reader's Digest Gardening Year*. He studied it avidly and started growing vegetables, wandering into the woods with a saw to cut hazel poles for his runner beans.

Birds were his passion. He had an aviary in the garden where he bred songbirds. But there was nothing he liked better than to go out nabbing pheasants with his dad. 'I remember when I was as young as six or seven, my mum waking us up at four in the morning, and we'd get into the blue fibreglass invalid car, and I'd be sat on the little toolbox next to my dad, and we'd go hurtling into the countryside, aiming to kill as many pheasants as we could. At night-time after a warmish day insects are attracted to the warm tarmac and the birds come down and feed on them. As soon as we saw one he'd turn the headlights on full glare and charge at them – I'd jump out of the car and whack 'em with my cosh if they were still moving. We wouldn't go home till we had four or five pheasants in the sack. We'd creep in at dawn and Mum would hang them up in the garage: one for the vicar, one for the social worker, and I felt like Robin Hood.'

Hollyhocks have been grown in London since medieval times — but perhaps not on a roof.

Aged twelve, he would rise at midnight and cycle through the night to search for birds' eggs, risking his neck clambering up trees and abseiling down cliff faces, once even breaking into a military camp and swimming naked across a lake to secure the treasured eggs of the crested grebe. 'It was the thrill of the hunt, but it was also about being out in the countryside and roaming; I could talk for hours about the eggs I found.' Even now, you can show him any egg, and he can tell you which bird laid it, and how and where it nests.

So Paul looked back over the wreckage of his life, and remembered the peace of the woods and the garden, and presented himself at nearby Spitalfields City Farm as a volunteer. 'They couldn't turn me down, because that's how city farms get their funding,' he says. 'I did all the digging and ground preparation for the Coriander Club [a community project for Asian women] and then that summer they won a prize for their vegetables and I thought: "Paul, that's your work there."'

Next, he applied to do an NVQ in conservation work, learning all kinds of landscape skills. 'There were just twelve places — me, another bloke and ten yummy mummies.' With them he discovered Tower Hamlets Cemetery Park —

an otherworldly island of urban woodland on the site of one of the great Victorian cemeteries of London, where he also volunteered on Fridays and Sundays. The yummy mummies loved him — he would thrill them in the minibus with hair-raising tales of his disreputable drug-fuelled past.

'To come off the heroin is the most horrific thing,' he says baldly, without self-pity. 'There's not many people that manage it — less than 5 per cent. And most of them are on methadone for life. If you imagine the most ill that you've ever been, and times it by ten, by a hundred, that's what it feels like when you begin to withdraw from heroin, and that's just the beginning: it gets worse and worse and worse. It's like torture, and it lasts for days. The pain is unbearable, both physically and mentally.

'It was only when I stopped thinking about just me and started thinking about other people that my life started to change.'

'I had to keep moving all through the day — six, seven days a week, because my brain was still screaming for heroin. I was taking methadone, but your brain does not stop thinking about heroin for a second. I'm only just getting there now — it takes as long to come off as you were on it, and I stuck needles in my arm every day for seven years. It's a really full-on life being an addict, finding the money for heroin day after day, week after week: whether you steal, or sell drugs, or peddle *The Big Issue*; however you do it, you can never stop.' Finding himself unable to relax, he started building a garden at the Providence Row hostel where he was staying on Hackney Road. 'I'd finish the day's volunteering and then go out collecting wood from skips to build raised beds. Everyone thought I was mad, out in that courtyard, full of dog shit. They'd say: "What are you doing out there? Building coffins?"'

His key worker supported him, and gave him money for soil. Then one by one, people started coming out to help, quietly, without saying much. Within a month they were producing their first veg. And Paul began to notice how much calmer he felt, and how his methadone dosage was coming down week by week.

The pace never slackened. Paul created a new wildlife garden at Spitalfields that won second prize in Hackney in Bloom 2005. On Sundays he worked with young offenders. And as the hostel gardeners ran out of space in the courtyard, they took over an allotment by the railway line. Then they built a wildlife garden for a local school. Sometimes there would be five of them, sometimes ten, sometimes more. He called his group 'Grounded', because that was how he felt.

'I knew immediately that everything I was doing — working at the farm, gardening, volunteering — was healing me. I'm working seven days a week because

Paul in the rooftop woodland grove, an extension of the garden which combines logs with living woodland plants.

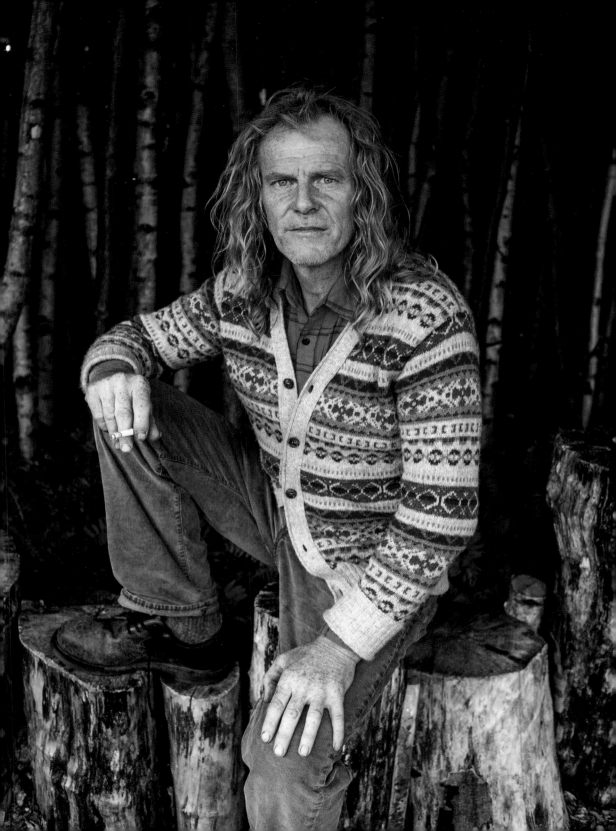

the monkey's still on my back, but loving every minute of it, because I've gone back to being a child and it's like going out to play every day. And suddenly I notice that all this shit that's been in my head for years and years and years is starting to go away. And I know now that what I'm doing — working with nature, hands in the soil, is what I'm meant to do on this earth.' Even astrologically, it seems a good fit. 'I'm Virgo so I'm an earth person,' Paul explains. 'I'm a rat in Chinese astrology and rats cannot be indoors. And now this thing I'm experiencing of being grounded is being handed on to other people.'

The next step, with the support of his mental health worker Kelvin Barton, was to take Grounded to the cemetery park to volunteer. It's no joke, Paul observes wryly, being responsible for up to a dozen smack-heads — people still on crack or trying to come off it, people with acute mental health problems, volatile and unpredictable, to whom you've just handed out axes and knives. But being out all day in the woods seemed to have an incredibly steadying effect. Paul's theory is that it calls to the inner caveman in us all. Or maybe it's simply that we're never too old to play in the woods — kicking leaves, chopping wood, cooking over open fires. Paul took a green woodworking course, won funding for tools, and began to share his new skills. And bit by bit, Grounded was asked to take on new projects in the community.

'All we really want is to go out to play. All this is playing — woodcrafts, carpentry, throwing earth around, growing things, all playing.'

Its big break came in 2009, when the Eden Project (an educational charity best known for its huge biomes in Cornwall), working in conjunction with various prisons and homeless groups, created the 'Key Garden' at the Chelsea Flower Show. Grounded was invited to work on the build, impressing all with their competence and commitment. The following year Eden secured funding for the Places of Change Garden, the biggest garden ever made at the show, again working with homeless and mental health charities. It was to be divided into five zones, and Paul was invited to design one of them, on the theme of recycling and conservation. Drawing on his group's experience at the cemetery park, Paul suggested a bodger's camp, built entirely with recycled wood and planted with British wild flowers. All the wood came from the park; the flowers they grew on from plugs in makeshift nurseries at Providence Row Housing Association properties around the East End. In fact, the most expensive part of the garden was the hire of the lorry to move their materials across London. It was a runaway success, and attracted masses of media attention. Paul took to the airwaves like a duck to water. 'I'm buzzing my tits off — this is fucking brilliant — this is *Chelsea* — and I'm there telling all these old colonels I used to be a heroin addict and they're all in awe ... And then I'm on

Paul is tickled by the irony that a site tended by recovering alcoholics and substance abusers is now one of the coolest places in London to enjoy a drink.

Radio Four and on *Gardeners' World* talking to millions of people about gardening for wildlife, how we must plant for the bees and the butterflies. And then they ask me to meet the Queen!'

Only Paul never did get to meet the Queen. At the time he was required to be filmed showing her around his garden, he had to go and pick up his script for Subutex (an opium-based painkiller which is a step on from methadone) – an appointment more urgent than even a royal command. So Paul had to watch, seething, on the television while someone from another homeless group walked Her Majesty through his garden. Even now you can see the anguish in his eyes.

By this time, Paul had won the respect of Eden's horticulturists and designers, so when, in 2011, London's Southbank Centre approached the Eden Project to create a sustainable roof garden, they at once asked Grounded to build it. The garden was built from scratch, using tons of gravel, sand and logs – some recycled from the Chelsea garden. It opened to the public from May to September, as part of the centre's anniversary celebrations, marking sixty years since the Festival of Britain.

At the same time, the Grounded team was awarded an 'Ecominds' grant, which encourages people affected by mental health issues to get involved in the great outdoors. This meant Paul could finally be paid for his work and earn a living as a professional gardener, moving out of the hostel and into his own flat. 'I'm poor as a church mouse,' he reflects, 'but I'm rich in other ways. This', he says, gesturing around him at the garden on Queen Elizabeth Hall, 'is pure magic. I've built a piece of countryside on top of a roof next to the River Thames. This is my Shangri-La.'

The entrance to the garden on the South Bank.

The road to Shangri-La has been a cruel one, but Paul firmly believes it is his karma, the path he was destined to follow. His adoptive father died when Paul was fourteen; by sixteen he was in with the wrong crowd. He left school; trained, improbably, as a hairdresser; then a girlfriend persuaded him to go to college for A levels. But these were the days before the Education Maintenance Allowance (since scrapped) and the bus fare and the college canteen soon proved beyond the family's means. So he got a job selling books door to door. Always one with the gift of the gab, he was brilliant at it, making so much money that he bought himself a sports car. Then he and his girlfriend went to Ibiza for the summer, and he smoked his first joint in the Café del Mar. He went back a second year, and developed a speed habit, which he financed by dealing drugs. He was good at selling them too. He made a heap of money, then had it ripped off him by villains rather bigger than he was. He travelled to India, Thailand, South America, ingesting every pharmaceutical he could lay his hands on. Then, in 1988 and the ecstasy-fuelled summer of love, Paul went out and hit the London club scene with all the skills he'd learned in Ibiza. He made stacks of cash again, lost it again, had a breakdown, went back to his mum, got clean.

What he didn't know then was that he was suffering from undiagnosed bipolar disorder, self-medicating with drugs during the downers. In the 1990s he made a decent and legitimate living, buying jewellery and textiles in India and selling them at markets and festivals. But India was to prove his undoing: in a cave in Dharamsala he discovered opium. As he tells it now, he was the wide-eyed innocent – getting on a plane home, thinking he had malaria, not understanding why he felt so ill, being rushed from Heathrow in an ambulance, not realizing he was an addict going cold turkey. Once he knew, it was a slippery slope to heroin and the street.

'I know now it's my karma because I never got caught and never went to prison. Everyone gets caught in the end, but I didn't. Living on the street was payback time for all the harm I did. Now it's all finally come together. I totally understand myself now; I can finally understand what's going on up here. It's all wonderful. I was depressed for years, but now I wake up happy every day because I'm helping other people. And I know the secret of a good life.'

Today Paul Pulford is a man on a mission, or rather several missions. 'I want to help people get over their mental health problems. To get people gardening to heal them is a no-brainer. Not everyone is my group is a natural, passionate gardener; but to feel something alive, whether tree or soil, to be outside, to get out in the woods, is to experience something real, to get back in touch with where we came from. This concrete jungle around us isn't reality.'

He worries desperately about generations of urban children brought up without that essential, visceral experience. 'There are so many kids now who've never made dens or climbed trees, or gone down the park to play football with their mates. All they know is their little screens . . .' How, he wonders, is a generation so deeply dissociated from the planet ever to be galvanized to care for it? 'It's the kids who have to end the cycles of destruction – it's no good relying on sad old hippies like me.'

Nonetheless, Paul feels satisfied he is making a difference. The Queen Elizabeth Hall garden was supposed to last just for the summer, but proved so popular it remained in place for Southbank Centre's 'Festival of the World' in 2012, its veg beds showcasing exotic varieties from all corners of the globe. In 2013 it expanded on to the roof of the Hayward Gallery in a series of shady tunnels and woodland glades. In creating a mini nature reserve on what was a barren rooftop, and in other projects such as making wildlife gardens in schools and planting new banks of wild flowers in East London's Victoria Park, he feels he's putting a modest stamp on the world.

'My interest in gardening is in using only British wild flowers and herbs, because I then know that, while I'm gardening and giving pleasure to myself, I am also doing it for the planet, for the bees and the butterflies, and that makes me feel good. I don't know a roof anywhere in the country that's as species-rich as this one.' He has even made a mini wetland to accommodate various bog-loving plants, along with pockets of crushed limestone for calcicolous grassland species and special niches for favourite rarities like bladder campion. On the walls are chalked lists of birds and butterflies spotted in the garden. All kinds of invertebrates scuttle in the bark mulch, and toads and shrews are nesting under the logs. Next year he's hoping to draft in the Natural History Museum – aided, of course, by a workforce of children – to count up all the different species.

For Kelvin, who still pitches up at least once a week, the significance of the garden is rather different. He values it as a place where people with various mental health problems can come together to share experiences and support each other, an arena where they can talk openly and not feel excluded, and, most importantly, a place where they can interact with the public in a positive way, rather than feeling invisible or in some way embarrassing.

'What makes me happiest is working with the earth, working with nature, being passionate about wanting to turn people on to gardening with wild flowers. Getting people to realize, this guy, he's telling it like it is.'

Paul is immensely proud that Grounded has already paved the way back into work for four of its members, now all gainfully employed as gardeners. Making the garden, people who hadn't worked for years turned up sober every day for five weeks, worked all day in the hot sun for not a penny, and created a work of beauty. It gave them a purpose, a huge and unfamiliar sense of achievement, even a new identity – no longer just drunks or dropouts, but gardeners. The group went on to cement their credentials by taking the horticulture course at the Eden Project, approved by the Royal Botanic Garden Edinburgh. Every one of them passed.

'I have a piece of paper now that proves I'm a gardener,' marvels Paul. He even got to grips with horticultural Latin. Right now, though, he's preoccupied by a problem that wasn't on the syllabus – how to manage the four Guernsey goats he has just let loose on the rooftop as an eco-friendly alternative to the strimmer. Then, splendidly, Paul's dog Scruffy takes charge, snapping at their fluffy heels.

Paul beams. 'My life is wonderful; knackering, but wonderful. I'm always going at a thousand miles an hour – I don't have time to be depressed. I'm being the nature warden I wanted to be, but I have the opportunity to talk to loads more people, to try to turn them on to what's in my head. It's a simple message – enjoy gardening, enjoy growing your vegetables, but remember the wildlife around you. If something doesn't offer anything to nature, do without it. This is me paying back nature for all those eggs I stole.'

OPPOSITE, ABOVE *Goats from a nearby city farm offer a green alternative to a strimmer when the beds need clearing – or at least, that's the theory.*
OPPOSITE, BELOW *Paul with his best friend, Scruffy.*

BUT IS IT ART?

MICK EVANS
Packwood House, Warwickshire

*'I want you to get the feeling of walking in amongst the plants
— that the plants are embracing you.'*

D EEP IN THE HEART of Shakespeare's Forest of Arden, improbably only eleven miles from the heaving centre of Birmingham, a narrow country lane meanders through the middle of a sixteenth-century rural estate, separating the gabled house from the stables and kitchen garden. The house has been through many changes: the original half-timbered structure extended with tawny brickwork in the seventeenth century, and plastered with a dingy grey render in the nineteenth. But the original garden layout remains largely intact — rectangular courts surrounding the house and a spiral mount to the south, crowned by a mighty yew. This, both literally and symbolically, is the high point of a venerable topiary garden, long believed to represent the Sermon on the Mount. For generations, this grave and shadowy garden was Packwood's sole claim to fame. But look in the National Trust guidebook now and all that has changed. There is a new orchard and a restored kitchen garden — some of it tended by local schools through the year. Visitor numbers have increased so much a visitor centre and tea room have been built. And what is packing them in more than anything is the spectacular new planting by head gardener Mick Evans, who has transformed Packwood's lacklustre herbaceous borders into high-adrenaline horticultural theatre.

'Mick Evans has done nothing less than invent a new style of planting for the twenty-first century,' says Mike Calnan, Head of Gardens at the National Trust, admiringly.

'I'd say that was going a bit far,' says Mick, his cheeks burning. We settle in the end for 'reinvention' — Mick will allow that he has taken a tradition of planting espoused by successive head gardeners at Packwood for over a century, and reinterpreted it for our times to create plantings of extraordinary energy, artistry and *joie de vivre*. The striking counterpoint between all this herbaceous juice and joy and the monochrome solemnity of the towering yews now makes Packwood a very rich garden indeed.

'Nothing is really new — this is the mingled style, but honed a little.'

Mick is a man with a deep feeling for history: it is vivid and present to him. He drives an old Royal Enfield, wearing an open-faced helmet and goggles. He treasures wartime sketches made by his father — hastily snatched studies of troops sailing off to war. At Packwood, it was the historic fabric that drew him to the place: the frivolous gazebos in the corners of the gardens; the muddle of rosy outbuildings, mossy seventeenth-century brickwork pierced by bee boles; the ancient box hedge, scooped and puckered into armadillo folds.

Usually, garden historians are called in to help prepare management plans for National Trust properties. Mick and his wife, Tor, did the work themselves, poring over old maps and photographs, peeling back the layers to try to grasp the essence of the place. They found that the Sermon on the Mount story was a nineteenth-century invention; and that much of 'historic' Packwood was a fiction created by its last owner, Graham Baron Ash, who refashioned the house to make it ever grander and more romantic. He took a similar approach to the garden, deciding, in 1932, to create a 'Charles II' garden based, he claimed, on an unexecuted plan of 1677. This involved adding further gazebos, creating hedged rose beds and a sunken garden, and sweeping away existing herbaceous borders in favour of an elaborate box-edged parterre. This confection lasted barely a decade. As the supply of labour dwindled during the war, the parterre was grassed over, and so it remained until Mick appeared at Packwood.

This blank space troubled Mick and Tor, for what had been lost was the main axis of the garden, running from the house to the spiral mount. 'It's a fantastically powerful vista', insists Mick, 'which existed for centuries. But the connection between house and garden had been lost, so the house seemed to be floating on an island.' Eventually, they found a pair of photographs from 1927 that showed this axis as a wide gravel path flanked by crammed herbaceous borders. If Baron Ash could cherry-pick favourite moments in Packwood's history, why shouldn't Mick do the same?

PAGES 74–75 *The yew topiaries at Packwood, probably planted around 1650, have grown to a prodigious size in the Sermon on the Mount garden.*
OPPOSITE *There is much to be done before the garden opens each day.*

Cool plantings of Strobilanthes atropurpurea *frame an ornate ironwork gateway out to the park.*

It took four years to persuade the Trust to reinstate these borders – years Mick spent researching the plant lists of former head gardeners and thinking about how they should be planted. Until 1941, when Ash handed over the house to the National Trust, Packwood had adopted the 'mingled' style of planting. This is a term coined by the nineteenth-century gardening guru John Claudius Loudon, who continued to dominate the theory and practice of gardening long after his death in 1843. In his *Encyclopædia of Gardening* of 1822, Loudon categorizes flower gardens in three 'classes': mingled, select and changeable. The select garden depends on plants of one kind, as in a rose garden; the changeable garden consists chiefly of containers. The 'mingled' class is what most gardeners aspire to – combining plants so as to 'present a gay assemblage of flowers of different colours during the whole season'. Loudon recommends 'such plants as produce large heads, or masses of flowers', chosen 'without much regard to variety of form or diversity of character' and planted in equal numbers of each colour. He provides detailed instructions on how to produce a vivid show from February to October. 'It was a riot of really hot, bright colours', explains Mick, 'in small groups repeated along the borders, and with no distinction between one border and the next. Almost like an Edwardian bedding scheme, but done in perennials rather than annuals.'

Stipa gigantea *adds lightness to sultry borders flanking the restored axis to the house.*

Mick had something more sophisticated in mind — a planting style that still depended on the regular repetition of core groups of plants, but which took account of foliage and form as well as colour and which, most importantly, blended harmoniously into its surroundings. The new axial borders, created in 2006, use purples, maroons, and steely greys that flatter the ashen render of the house and are given lightness by a flutter of *Stipa gigantea* and mass by the statuesque forms of *Yucca recurvifolia*. 'They are fairly quiet colours', says Mick, 'that link to the house, the tiles and the copper beech in the distance. If you used a stronger palette against that rendering, it would almost seem as if the house were saying, "Don't look at me, I'm a bit of an ugly duckling." And we don't want that because the house is the heart of any garden, because everything emanates from that point. Look the other way, though, to the raised Terrace Walk, and there you can use bright, vibrant colours that play off the terracotta brickwork.'

Bright they certainly are. Mick savours the comment of garden critic Tim Richardson: 'One has heard the term "riot of colour" often enough in border descriptions; this border looks as if it might be about to start helping the police with their enquiries.' Yet for all the boldness, there is nothing harsh or jarring

Heleniums, fennel, crocosmias, Verbascum thapsus, Helianthus annuus *'Earth Walker' and, in the pot,* Agave americana.

— just a glorious sweep of scarlet crocosmias, golden sunflowers, chrome yellow achilleas, tawny heleniums and exuberant mounds of bright orange calendula spilling down the steps. 'Individually they might be quite distracting plants, but looking at the whole, there is a rhythm,' says Mick.

It's a powerful experience — enveloped in a corridor of colour, you push your way through overarching plants, dodge them, step around them. 'I want you to feel that the plants are embracing you,' says Mick. The cruel winter of 2010 robbed this border of many stars, especially mature phormiums and *Euphorbia mellifera*; but gradually the euphorbia is growing back, *Helianthus salicifolius* is adding height and the mahogany rosettes of *Aeonium* 'Zwartkop', which miraculously survived outdoor temperatures of −10°C, deliver a quirky muscularity. *Rosa moyesii*, planted to discourage children from climbing, dangles blood-red hips over the wall. 'Children run along the path sometimes, but they don't do a lot of damage. When I worked at Sissinghurst, keeping the paths clear of plants was always a priority, but if this was your garden, this is how you'd want it. I like to see plants have their character; I don't like things too neat and tidy.'

The hot borders riot over the paths running the length of the terrace between two brick pavilions.

What we see here is a style that bridges a century, taking Loudon's concept of repetition and infusing it with the looseness, rhythm and movement that characterizes the New Perennials style. Mick has also mastered the Sissinghurst trick of marrying billowing masses of planting with a tight formal architecture. Not that the children racing through the borders know that. They are far too busy playing hide and seek.

———◆———

'They fuck you up, your mum and dad.' Or, as Philip Larkin failed to observe, they can, just as inadvertently, be the making of you. Mick Evans always wanted to be an artist. But how could he ever live up to the talent of his father, a highly successful commercial artist whose almost photographic sleight of hand sang out from every bus and billboard throughout the 1960s? In the garden, though, father and son could meet on equal terms. They could share the enjoyment of gardening without expectation or pressure.

PAGES 82–83 *Rosy seventeenth-century brickwork frames the view through to the Sermon on the Mount garden.*

His father didn't push him. Mick had talent; but it was clear the days of illustration in advertising were numbered, and illustrating books was no way to feed a family. So Mick trained in horticulture instead. He didn't shine. Stuck in the classroom with an A3 sheet of squared paper, his attempts to design borders occasioned weary sighs and much rolling of eyes from his tutors. Still, they wrote him a reference for the local parks department, and by the time he was twenty-three Mick was the foreman.

Further promotion would have meant only incarceration in an office, so for six long years Mick stuck with it, working through every conceivable combination of bedding. All the while he was visiting gardens of distinction, looking, learning, hungry for a more creative form of horticulture, experimenting ceaselessly in his own small plot. At last, he knew exactly what he wanted: he applied for a job at Sissinghurst.

'I'm not very good at doing plans — I have to work it out as I'm going along. I can't get enthusiastic until I've got my hands in the soil — with me it takes the perspiration to generate the inspiration.'

Mick was under no illusions. 'They picked me because they needed someone physically strong. They needed someone to cut hedges and they knew I was good with lawns. I realized I had a lot to learn: that's where my gardening life truly started.'

When Mick arrived in 1989, the garden's creator, Vita Sackville-West, had been dead for twenty-seven years. It was really her 'Mädchen', head gardeners Pamela Schwerdt and Sibylle Kreutzberger, who had made Sissinghurst a byword for horticultural perfection — its pristine borders and laser-sharp hedges far more perfect, Nigel Nicolson observed, than anything that obtained in his parents' time.

'Pam and Sibylle were really tough taskmasters,' recalls Mick. 'Nobody new was going to do anything in the borders for at least a year; they needed to make sure that you were capable of working to their standards.' He spent his first year there following at their heels, listening as they spoke about colour; being taught how to look at all aspects of the garden, especially the architecture; how to make associations between plants and buildings; how to work every detail, right down to the colour of the lichen on the brick. 'I learned more from them in a month than three years at college,' he says. 'The delight of working at Sissinghurst — I'd have worked in the tea room — was being among people who were really enthused by their work; and that work was just a cut above anywhere else at that time — the detail, the standard of workmanship and the artistry. All of a sudden it clicked into place — that gardening could be art. It was a totally different form of art, but it *was* art.'

Dreamy hollyhock relative Althea cannabina *growing by the house.*

Mick spent two years with Pam and Sibylle. They would set him tests — identifying ten different clematis blooms, or articulating the difference between various shades of red — and Mick found he had inherited his father's fine appreciation of colour and form. After three further years with their successor, Sarah Cook, Mick felt he had served his apprenticeship, and sought out a new and very different mentor in Jimmy Hancock at Powis Castle in Wales.

'I was a bit in awe of Jimmy. The first thing he said was: "You can forget all your fancy Sissinghurst ideas. You'll learn to garden the Powis way and don't be too fussy: plants have to be able to express themselves."

'Jimmy had a far greater sense of freedom than I'd seen before. In a way, Pam and Sibylle played very safe — building layers of colour like painters, and using more "feminine" shades. Jimmy was far more random, far more experimental — much more willing to "suck it and see". So sometimes he made mistakes. You weren't allowed to do that at Sissinghurst — every week was Chelsea week. But in order to be able to move gardening on, even if just for your own pleasure, you have to be able to make mistakes, or all you can do is slavishly repeat what's gone before. Most new things that happen do so by accident.'

Hancock's questing vision and iconoclasm struck a chord with Mick. And at Powis, an outward-looking garden that exploits its dramatic topography to full advantage, he learned to work on a bolder, more panoramic scale. When Hancock retired, Mick was expected to apply for his post. Yet once again, he proved reluctant to follow the obvious path. 'Powis was Jimmy's garden. He'd created this wonderful balance between the natural and the formal, and I couldn't see how I could improve on that.'

Instead he started looking for somewhere he could make his mark. In 1999, Packwood was a backwater, but that meant it was ripe for innovation.

'Gardeners are not well-paid people, so the only thing that will keep you enthusiastic about what you do is trying to develop new ideas and new ways of doing things.'

A rudimentary seventeenth-century barometer is made of pine cones, which open and close more tightly according to the weather.

The downside of being an innovator is the pressure to keep on coming up with new tricks, pulling rabbits out of hats, year in, year out. So far, in addition to his contemporary mingled borders, Mick has redeveloped Packwood's sunken garden into a dry garden inspired by Beth Chatto, where some unusual plants can be enjoyed at close quarters; he has softened the West Court with self-seeding grasses and perennials; embellished the North Court with exotic foliage and turned a derelict kitchen garden into a simulacrum of a seventeenth-century gentleman farmer's plot. Then there's the small matter of maintaining a historically significant topiary garden: the yews alone take two and a half months to clip.

'Sometimes you beat yourself up and think you must always be doing something new,' says Mick. 'But ideas have to be sustainable – they can't be five-minute wonders. There are those electrifying moments when I'm doing some planting, and all of a sudden inspiration strikes and I have to act on it there and then; but generally ideas take time to develop, and I have to go away and cogitate until I understand them fully myself.

'With gardening, a lot of it is driven by your own motivation – you have to be always ready and firing, and though I love it, sometimes I get exhausted and wonder what it's all for.'

The kitchen garden is worked by local primary schools, who have contributed a splendid range of scarecrows to protect their crops.

It's at times like these that he picks up his brushes: his office, which curiously resembles a ship, is lined with studies of flowers. It's hard to believe that someone who wields colour with such confidence and exuberance can be prey to periods of depression. There is solace in this miniaturist, private art, which can exist, as it were, in a vacuum. Gardening, by contrast, he sees as 'a three-dimensional art form of which you, the viewer, form part – it exists all around you and relies on your senses to be appreciated.' The interplay between artist and viewer is essential to him: acutely aware how gardens change day by day and year by year, he remains as anxious about his work as a playwright on opening night, waiting heart-in-mouth for his reviews. Gardening is generally an opinionated business, with little time for constructive criticism, so such humility is rare. He might not necessarily agree, but he listens, carefully. Though he obviously takes delight in plaudits from gardening's great and good, a moment he seems to cherish above all is when a visitor in Lycra cycle shorts abruptly announced that he wasn't a gardener, didn't like gardening and yet found himself curiously moved and excited by the planting of the Terrace Walk: proof positive, to Mick's mind, that a garden can aspire to the condition of art.

'I find it very hard to follow other people, to stick to their rules — once I have the basic knowledge to follow my own instincts, that works much better.'

Sometimes Mick dreams of starting again with a clean sheet — somewhere sheltered and mild, in the South West, where he could grow the semi-tender subshrubs he especially enjoys. (He adores Tresco Abbey Garden on the Isles of Scilly.)

'I know this sounds funny, but I would love to work with an owner who just wants to create something new — who would allow me to start again with a blank sheet in a derelict garden with a history. When I was younger, I wanted to impress, but now I just want to see what I can do with what I've learned. It would be enough to be able to earn a living, creating something very beautiful, and not to do what everyone expects. My father always said, if you have a talent, you must see where it takes you.'

With such energy, such passion and such openness to experience, there is surely a long and exciting road ahead.

National Trust

GARDEN TALKS
THURSDAYS
at 3 p.m.

19th Sept: The Kitchen Garden
26th Sept: The Sunken Garden
3rd Oct: Trimming formal hedges
10th Oct: The Kitchen Garden

GARDENING LIKE A COW

BEATRICE KREHL
Waltham Place, Berkshire

*'If we want to survive, we have to stop pretending we know it all,
and try to learn more from nature. We have to be much
more observant, and much more humble.'*

BEATRICE KREHL is considered by many in the gardening world to be
stark, staring mad. She has become used to garden visitors angrily demanding
their money back, and frequently has to dash to stop others, in the spirit of
kindness, tearing up the plants (aka weeds) she has carefully nurtured.

For this is a woman who actually plants bindweed – who, rather than rushing
out with trowel and Roundup anxious to release its stranglehold on its neighbours,
has spent years trying to coax it to twine up bamboo poles. (It won't, of course –
you can always rely on bindweed for sheer cussedness.)

She also embraces ground elder – a most attractive ground cover, in her opinion,
that looks particularly lovely flowering between 'Nevada' roses. In fact, there is a
whole section of her garden where ground elder is king. 'I don't see it as a terrible
enemy – I see it as my first vegetable in spring,' says Beatrice. 'I am always happy when
the new, young leaves appear in March and April. I cut them up finely and use them
in soups and salads, with a mixture of nettle, lovage and sorrel. They're also very
nice with wild garlic. At that time, you don't have many fresh greens in the kitchen
garden, so it's very welcome. You just need to look at the plant a little differently.'

As for bindweed, no one can deny it is beautiful. It was always a source of
puzzlement to Beatrice's South African employer, Strilli Oppenheimer, that British
gardeners should prize the morning glories from the land of her birth, yet declare

war on their no less lovely cousin. When Oppenheimer decided to redevelop the somewhat run-down garden at their home at Waltham Place in Berkshire in 1999, a key part of her brief was that the existing weeds should be maintained. Her aim was to garden in harmony with nature – to combine forces with the indigenous flora and fauna rather than fighting against them, and to explore the boundaries between garden and nature.

It is an aim with which Beatrice is in perfect accord. 'A garden shouldn't be a battleground. I find it very disturbing that 90 per cent of the questions asked in a garden are: "What are you doing against slugs/blackfly/greenfly/ground elder/ bindweed?" – as if it were a war zone. 'I'm trying to show that if you shift your mindset, you just don't see these things as a problem any more.'

In the walled Square Garden at Waltham Place, an exuberant planting of glorious thugs has lived in cheerful accord with ground elder for a decade or more: phloxes, Korean feather reed grass (*Calamagrostis brachytricha*), meadow rue (*Thalictrum aquilegiifolium*), *Calamagrostis* × *acutiflora* 'Karl Foerster', great fluffy clumps of *Persicaria alpina* (syn. *polymorpha*) and the statuesque giant umbellifer *Peucedanum verticillare*. ('The first year it makes its leaves; the second year it makes a telegraph pole,' says Beatrice admiringly.) There are also some surprisingly dainty bedfellows. *Geranium psilostemon* and starry *Gillenia trifoliata* both seem to cope with no trouble at all, through Beatrice confesses to giving the astrantias a helping hand by 'gardening like a cow' – a delicious term coined by Dutch garden designer Henk Gerritsen. It means yanking out a handful of the weed when it threatens to overwhelm its neighbours, but without disturbing the soil. 'So you see there is a lot that can grow successfully,' insists Beatrice. 'There's no need to be so neurotic about it. Last year I found a bee orchid among the ground elder. We don't have them anywhere else on the estate, so I don't know how it got there.'

'Gardening like a cow' is the byword for most of the borders, and especially in the New Garden, where couch grass constantly threatens to overwhelm the small, fingernail-shaped beds, despite the attentions of muntjacs, rabbits and real cows leaning over the fence. Only the potager is more exclusively managed, in order to make space for less resilient cutting annuals.

Our attitude to weeds, thinks Beatrice, is generally barbaric. In Germany, with its well-established tradition of naturalistic planting, it is a great deal more sophisticated. By selecting cultivated plants that are vigorous self-seeders, or which are tolerant of various stress factors (more so than most weeds), or which 'have elbows', like the robust plantings in Waltham's Square Garden, it is possible to create self-sustaining, naturalistic plantings that can get by with a minimum of intervention. This, Beatrice stresses, is a quite different thing from neglect and

The New Garden was originally intended for bearded iris, but proved too wet. Now it is stocked with wet meadow plants such as Iris sibirica, Deschampsia *and devil's-bit scabious* (Succisa pratensis), *and gardened 'like a cow'.*

actually requires much deeper plant knowledge: the ability to tell a weedling from a seedling, to know just how it will grow and to what size. Beatrice weeds, but you can't tell she's weeded. 'I see myself as a sculptress of green mass; going through day by day and deciding what to take out and what to leave. It's a very dynamic process because it is never two years the same. I like that. The traditional border with drifts of plants is far simpler to maintain – there is this block and the next block and everything in between can go. When it's finished, it looks like a catastrophe – all that bare ground.' She actually shudders. 'Nature doesn't do bare ground – I try to keep it covered.'

———✦———

Beatrice never trained as a gardener. But she grew up in a garden – her mother was a keen vegetable grower – and she was always interested in plants. At her childhood home, just north of Lucerne in Switzerland, she spent long days roaming the meadows – in those days still rich in wild flowers – and making gardens in the neighbouring woodlands.

PAGES 94–95 *The tidiest and most conventional of the gardens at Waltham Place.*

'As a child I was always transplanting things in the woods – digging up oxslips and moving them somewhere else,' she says. 'I liked to be out in nature, so when I had to go to school for seven years I thought that was a real waste of time.'

Despite her initial reluctance, Beatrice did well and went on to university. At first it was a toss-up whether to work with animals or plants, so she decided to train as an agronomist – until she discovered landscape architecture. 'I wasn't quite sure what it was, but it seemed to be a little bit of farming, architecture, art, biology, botany, ecology – all things that were very interesting to me.' It also introduced her to garden design. 'In our garden at home, we had only ever thought about production, never about how it looked. It was a big eye-opener for me to find out about modern art and architecture.' She is full of admiration for her professor, the late Dieter Kienast (best known in Britain for his landscaping around Tate Modern), and his aesthetic of bringing nature into the city. And, above all, she loved the botanizing, setting off into the Swiss Alps, looking for plants. 'I still think plants in the wild are the most beautiful. In a garden, very often you will see plants together and think, "Oh dear, those are ugly plants." But they are not

For Beatrice, gardening is all about living on easy terms with nature.

ugly, they are just in the wrong position, or used the wrong way. In nature, the combinations are always right.'

On graduating, she got a job in a design office and, as a beginner, it was her job to work on the planting. It both amused and frustrated her that planting design was held in such low regard. More frustrating still was the fact that there was never time to see a garden develop. 'Just as the garden is beginning to get interesting, you move on to the next one. And I felt more and more that I was lacking experience with plants.'

'One lifetime is not enough for a gardener to learn everything.'

When, in the 1990s, the local economy collapsed (Beatrice ascribes it to new Swiss money laundering regulations), she was left jobless and signed up for a course in environmental design in the Netherlands. It proved a life-changing decision, not so much because of her studies, but because, in 1996, she volunteered at Dedemsvaart, home of garden design legend Mien Ruys. Here, at the family nursery famous throughout Europe for its perennials, Ruys had created a series of demonstration gardens that effectively chart the history of garden design from the 1920s onwards, which combined rigorous architectural form with increasingly naturalistic planting. The gardens showed clearly the transition from the big, country house gardens to small, urban gardens; how Ruys had embraced new materials from concrete to recycled plastic; and, in the blocks of planting contrasting with simple, straight lines, the influences she had taken from functionalist architects and the Bauhaus.

After just a week, one of the gardeners went off sick, so Beatrice finished the season for her. She ended up staying for nine years. 'I'd had the illusion that I could learn all about perennial plants in a single season – seventy years' experience in one summer!' she laughs. 'Until then I had been interested only in natives – I had a very rigid approach to planting. What happened there was that I began to learn more about cultivated plants: the peonies, then the delphiniums, and so on. At first it was just the herbaceous plants that interested me; then the bulbs; then the annuals and shrubs ... As Mien always said, "One lifetime is not enough for a gardener to learn everything."'

In 1996, the *grande dame* of European garden design was already ninety-two years old. In the evenings she would sit in the garden with her G&T (all G, no T), and Beatrice would listen to her stories. 'She had worked everywhere, and known everyone. She had met Gertrude Jekyll and visited her at Munstead Wood. In the 1930s she was in Berlin, when German nurseryman Karl Foerster was very active. She went to see *The Threepenny Opera* and met Bertolt Brecht – she always said that turned her into a socialist. Well before the Second World War she already could see that the Netherlands stood between the German and English gardening traditions, and could develop a uniquely interesting garden architecture. But after the war, no one else wanted to know about the German ecological tradition. Everyone then was worshipping Sissinghurst and Hidcote.'

Then in the 1990s, shortly before Beatrice arrived at Dedemsvaart, things suddenly began to change. All at once she found herself at the epicentre of the Dutch New Wave – a new approach to perennial planting espoused by pioneers such as Piet Oudolf and Henk Gerritsen. 'It was Mien, really, who started off the new perennials movement,' says Beatrice. 'It was at Dedemsvaart that Henk Gerritsen understood that you could use plants in garden settings: before that he was only interested in plants in the wild.'

Gerritsen is the other great influence in Beatrice's gardening life. He designed the garden at Waltham Place for Strilli Oppenheimer, and it

'In nature there are all these self-controlling circles. If we get in trouble with pests, for example, it's usually us who are to blame. Usually the plants eaten by slugs are just not very healthy: a slug is often a messenger that something else is wrong. Of course, I didn't like them eating my delphiniums – and in the first two or three seasons it was very difficult to get them through. But now they're fine. And when I see aphids on my vegetables, I know the ladybirds aren't very far behind.'

was he who lured Beatrice to England to manage it. They did not, initially, hit it off. 'When Henk went to Dedemsvaart, his first response was, "I can do better,"' recalls Beatrice. 'Mine was, "I can learn." I think that illustrates our different characters.'

Gerritsen, in his *Essay on Gardening*, written shortly before his death in 2008, acknowledges the 'slap in the face' of his visit to Dedemsvaart in 1977: 'this was art. I had never realized that something like that was possible with plants.' To his mind, though, Mien Ruys's plantings were not nearly wild enough. This incensed Beatrice: Gerritsen seemed to be criticizing plantings pioneering in their time but made half a century earlier. What would people say of Gerritsen's own plantings in fifty years' time? She knew his garden at Priona, in the north-east of the Netherlands, well – a garden that walked the most precarious tightrope between the cultivated and the wild. Beatrice is neat by nature, and Gerritsen's embrace of 'failure' – insect damage, rot, collapse and death, which left leaves munched to doilies and stalks reduced to mush – was hard to stomach. The strenuous quirkiness of his topiary and garden ornament could be grating, too. But these two feisty characters shared a vision – of gardens that truly respected the cycles of nature, furnished with naturalistic plantings which were less about artistic arrangements of flowers than creating communities of plants that could live together successfully, without violence to other living things. A garden is a work of artifice, and can therefore never be entirely 'wild' – but if a gardener could willingly accept time and change and happenstance, relinquishing the desire to subdue nature to her will, that would be the next best thing.

Beatrice had spent years preaching that English gardens were dull and dated, even uttering the heresy that Sissinghurst was boring. Now, here she was on a plane for the first time in her life, acutely uncomfortable at the expanse of fresh air between herself and the soil, bound for an interview in Cape Town, to take charge of a garden in the English Home Counties designed by a Dutchman and with an agenda entirely different from any other garden in Britain.

Coming to England was not easy. Beatrice got on famously with her new employer – they share a passion for cows. But then Oppenheimer is not English.

'Nobody told me how difficult the English are; how they don't say what they mean,' says Beatrice. 'It was a real culture shock. Coming from the Netherlands, I had a bit of a handicap. I had been living with artists, and was used to people being direct. I wasn't expecting to have to learn to read between the lines. Of course,

In the Butterfly Garden, Coreopsis tripteris *provides a delicate frame for artwork by Roger Doyle.*

I made huge mistakes,' she sighs. 'I trampled on many toes, because I just said what I thought. People thought I was shockingly rude, but no one ever said anything, so it took me years to find out.'

To add to the difficulties of that first year (2005), she was obliged to work alongside the head gardener she would be replacing. His task had been to put Gerritsen's redesign in place; Beatrice's role was now to develop and refine the garden. And although that had always been understood, it was still difficult for a gardening professional to see himself replaced by a sprig of a girl without a day's horticultural training. Nor did she always approve of what had been done: in the Long Border, for example, long-established plantings which had successfully withstood the depredations of rabbits and deer had been swept away wholesale, providing a banquet of vulnerable young plants. A decade on, she is still trying to make good this folly.

'I really love cattle. As a child I always wanted my own zoo, with all different cattle breeds.'

There were practical difficulties too. Gerritsen's plant palette, sourced mainly from the towering Piet Oudolf, tends to the lofty – and Beatrice is only just five feet tall. Cutting back massive yew hedges, or wading in to clear deep ponds, proved something of a physical challenge. Not driving in an area lacking in rural transport was also an issue. Fortunately, she is largely self-sufficient, growing her own vegetables and making her own sourdough bread and yoghurt with milk from the estate's Jersey cows.

<small>FROM LEFT TO RIGHT *Beatrice's beloved Jersey cows. The pot store. Simple hedged ovals of turf placed at intervals in the Long Border give breathing space between dense masses of planting.*</small>

She feels, on the whole, that her lack of formal training makes her more open to experimentation. But not always. On one occasion, Gerritsen decided that they would do no cutting back in spring, just to see what happened. 'It was a bit like torture,' recalls Beatrice. 'The insects were happy, but it was hellish for the gardeners, trying to deal with new growth coming through the old.' Then there was the fact that Beatrice was far more interested in food-growing than Gerritsen, who enjoyed vegetables primarily for their flowers.

Every year Gerritsen would come to clip the hedges himself (especially his signature 'caterpillar' hedge in the Square Garden) and to pronounce on the garden. But one year he ran out of time and Beatrice had to finish them herself. Rather to her surprise, she passed muster. 'The first year he wasn't too impressed with me. Now he decided I must stay here till I drop.'

⊷×⊶

At Waltham Place, organic management is not so much a set of techniques as a belief system. The garden forms part of a 220-acre organic and biodynamic farm of which about forty acres is woodland, another forty arable, and the remainder is pasture, supporting a herd of forty cows, two flocks of sheep (Jacobs and Castlemilk Moorits), pigs and poultry. The garden takes its place in a circular, self-sufficient system which might seem ludicrously old-fashioned to agribusiness, but which is, Beatrice firmly believes, the only viable way forward.

She is horrified at genetic modification, aghast at lab-created meat, and no less so at the waste inherent in modern conventional farming. 'They say organic farming can't feed the world, but in fact nothing else can, because conventional farming is so heavily reliant on fossil fuels, which are a finite resource. The only way is to work with nature with holistic management techniques. If we destroy the soil with fertilisers — and people already knew this was happening right back in the 1920s — we've had it. Both successful farming and successful gardening depend on looking after the soil.'

To this end, Beatrice and her team produce some fifteen tons of compost every year, mixing garden waste with animal manure and woodchip from the woodlands. There's far more than can go on the vegetable gardens — the ornamental borders are kept lean — so it is brewed into compost teas that are spread on the fields.

'I am a very convinced organic gardener,' she declares. 'I have never used pesticides. I have never wanted to poison things. I can't see the point.' She finds it disturbing that so many conservationists here embrace herbicides — that the common advice for establishing a wild flower meadow or organic veg plot is to first spray with glyphosate and to start with a clean sheet. 'Clean' is a handy euphemism for 'dead', she points out. How can that be right?

Beatrice and Logan take a break in the garden's tree house.

'We don't really understand the complex systems of nature. We just mess up, over and over again. There is a poem of Goethe's that is always in my ears: *The Sorcerer's Apprentice* – he knew only how to start the spell, but not how to stop it. It's the same with us. We've learned part of a trick, and we think we're so clever, and then we make a mess. If we want to survive, we have to stop pretending we know it all, and try to learn more from nature. We have to be much more observant, and much more humble.'

The Oppenheimers had observed the success of biodynamic vineyards in South Africa, so, since 2005, the estate at Waltham Place has been managed biodynamically. It was a new technique to Beatrice, but she has taken to it, particularly the organization of garden tasks according to the lunar calendar. She enjoys the structure it provides, though tying it in with weather conditions can be a challenge, particularly on their heavy clay soil. Her highest priority in the garden is growing vegetables, and she is convinced that the vegetables produced in this way are superior, in vigour and size as well as flavour, to those produced by an organic regime alone.

Beatrice is also deeply involved in the work of the farm, particularly with her beloved Jersey cows. A Saturday is more likely to find her crooning at fluffy, Bambi-eyed calves or leading a well-brushed heifer round the show ring than garden visiting or, heaven forfend, shooting up to London. She's a country girl at heart, and though she's sociable and chatty, she has no yearning for the bright lights. 'I have my dog,' she says, and seems content. 'Everything I need is here.' (It is notable that terrier Logan is not left in a state of nature, but meticulously trimmed, with not a hair out of place.)

On the one hand, then, her horizons are exceedingly narrow. On the other, they could scarcely be wider. With the Oppenheimers, she travels regularly to Africa, and has had the chance to explore all kinds of techniques from holistic grazing management to traditional Japanese gardening. Her greatest joy has been the discovery of true wilderness. Brought up in the shadow of the mountains, she had always been acutely aware of the force and majesty of nature. But 'in Europe, there is no wilderness left,' she says. 'What we call nature is always culture. In Africa, there are still pockets where you can see real wilderness. The experience has been humbling. We are not essential. We always think we are the pinnacle of evolution, but nature can do very well without us. It's a lesson I try to live by every day.'

While this book was in production, Beatrice moved on to pursue a freelance career in biodynamic growing. Waltham Place continues to be run on the same lines.

IS A MAN
UP TO THE JOB?

TROY SCOTT SMITH
Sissinghurst Castle, Kent

'People have gone off the idea that gardening is a slow process.
But it shouldn't be about instant gratification — the journey is also
important, enjoying the processes of change and replanting and renewal,
rather than waiting for some result that may never come.'

THERE ARE THOSE who say Troy Scott Smith has the best job in British
horticulture. He's in charge of the most famous garden in England, a byword
for horticultural excellence that is revered and emulated throughout the world. He
has a proficient and sufficient team, a high profile, ample funding, an enviable place
at the pinnacle of the horticultural establishment. He should be grateful.

There are also those who say Troy Scott Smith shouldn't be at Sissinghurst.

First, he's a man — a young(ish) family man seizing a baton that has been carefully
passed down through a succession of exceptional women gardeners. Wasn't there a
woman who could have filled the role?

And then he's a heretic. A precocious overachiever who was already a head
gardener at just twenty-five years old, he has cut a Byronic swathe through the
British horticultural establishment, a solitary figure who walks his own path, who is
confident in his own opinions, who is not afraid to blast a few sacred cows.

He's a man who says the unthinkable — or perhaps what everyone else is thinking
but doesn't dare speak. Sissinghurst, he says, has lost its way. In becoming a totem of
horticultural perfectionism, it has forgotten what it really is.

'For me gardens are a cycle,' he declares. 'Plants grow and they die during the
year. And gardens, over a period of years, also go up and down. So there's something

that disturbs me about trying to keep somewhere like Sissinghurst at this level all the time. Why not allow it just to fade and drop a little bit in places, because that's natural? It almost feels as if there's a tension there that doesn't sit easily …'

It's a statement that reveals the man. Take an iconic garden, lauded with every superlative in the lexicon, and decide it would be better if it were less, well, iconic. Do your job better by a bit of judicious slacking.

Troy is not a man uneasy with paradox. While he reveres the art of the garden, frankly, he'd rather spend his time out in the wilds. 'To see a mountain or a woodland or a natural meadow, even just a rock formation – the beauty of a landscape is far more nourishing for me. I could sit out here all morning looking at the view,' he says, gazing out over the Kentish Weald, 'but I'd probably get bored sitting in the rose garden for an hour.'

Gardens, he confesses, no longer move him – the shock and awe he experienced at the first sight of Powis or Rousham or Stourhead are long gone. And yet it's exactly that profound emotional experience that he wants to recreate at Sissinghurst. Too many visitors, he feels, are just ticking off a must-see garden. He wants to shake them to the core, so that they leave feeling thrilled, enriched, excited. 'And as they move through the garden's rooms, they should also feel warm and cosy and nourished – all those things you'd want to experience in a love affair. Of all the gardens I know, Sissinghurst is the one that should be giving rise to those sorts of feelings.'

How is it to be done? He is irritated by the 'ancestor worship' that pervades Sissinghurst, and yet there's no denying that Vita Sackville-West and Harold Nicolson, the creators of the garden, are the story here, and he constantly reads and rereads their writings as he wrestles to delineate the spirit of place. (Analysis, he observes, is a lot more interesting than weeding.)

He has known perfection in a garden, yet perceives the pursuit of it here as a dead weight crushing the life out of the garden's more elusive qualities. He wants to make his mark, but the measure of his success will be how completely he can inhabit the mind of a long-dead woman, to make the garden embody her vision once more.

＊

Poet, novelist, travel writer and muse; serial seducer of clever and beautiful women (not least Virginia Woolf); an aristocrat in love with her own history, debarred by her gender from inheriting the palace of Knole that was her childhood home: Vita Sackville-West would have ample claim to fame had she never picked up a trowel.

OPPOSITE *It was from Sissinghurst's romantic Elizabethan tower that Harold Nicolson laid out the garden, calling down instructions to his sons below, armed with canes and lengths of string.*
PAGES 110—111 *The notebooks of Vita Sackville-West and Harold Nicolson are Troy's constant study.*

Sissinghurst was very much a joint effort, Vita contributing the exuberant planting, as in her much-copied White Garden.

She was in many ways, the first modern media gardener, reaching a wide public through radio broadcasts and weekly columns in *The Observer*. And in her beloved garden at Sissinghurst, she perfected a style of garden rooms and colour-themed planting that continues to dominate garden design to this day. 'It's hard to think of a garden that has been more influential, or more widely copied,' says Mike Calnan, Head of Gardens at the National Trust, 'and not just in Britain. There are white gardens today on every continent – and even a complete Sissinghurst replica in Japan.'

Vita, however, is only half of the Sissinghurst legend. The garden owes just as much to her husband, Harold Nicolson, who created the confident geometry of garden rooms that frames Vita's romantic planting. It was Harold, armed with string and canes, who planted the hedges and created the vistas, who raised the walls and pierced the gateways that create Sissinghurst's playful magic. One room leads to another, enticing the visitor with glimpses of delights to come, luring us on through each succeeding portal, to ambush us there with some suddenly unfolding vista or unexpected set piece of planting.

It was Harold who laid out the clean geometric lines that give pace and structure to the garden, as in the Lime Walk.

Vita died in 1962, and the garden that exists today is substantially different from the one she left behind. Much was changed and adapted by Pam Schwerdt and Sibylle Kreutzberger, the pair of head gardeners Vita appointed in 1959, and who remained in charge when Sissinghurst passed to the National Trust ten years later. Sibylle has told Troy they were unimpressed by the garden, finding it messy and overgrown. But by the time they retired in 1991 they had turned Vita's romantically ramshackle garden into a beacon of horticultural precision. It was they who produced the razor-sharp hedges and pristine borders that they handed on to their protégée, Sarah Cook. She, in turn, handed over to her own chief assistant, Alexis Datta. There hasn't been a man in charge since Vita waved off her trusted retainer Jack Vass sixty years ago.

Troy claims to be gender blind. He doesn't believe there's such a thing as a male or female sensibility. There are just good and bad gardeners. He's more concerned with which of these layers of history constitute the 'authentic' Sissinghurst. Two-thirds of the plants now in the garden were added by Pamela and Sibylle, and both Sarah and Alexis have introduced new features. 'That has changed the character of the garden: it has elongated the season and added more interest. Or you could say that it's become a bit of a fruit salad, that you no longer get the one big climax that Vita so enjoyed because it's so diluted with other stuff. But it would be wrong simply to go back; gardens change.'

In some ways, he concedes, it's the least of his problems. By the gate is a blackboard indicating plants of interest. Chances are the plants featured there are not the most interesting at all. 'We have to be really careful. If we put something on there

which directs too many visitors to one spot, that spot gets worn out, and the plant gets picked to death.' In the rose garden, you can see all the places where the box hedges are bare and the underplanting worn away, where visitors have stepped close to smell a bloom. And some of the roses look distinctly peaky. It's not for want of care. 'I think I would get pretty tired if I was touched a thousand times a day,' sighs Troy. 'You do notice how plants can look quite stressed on a

A blackboard in the entrance directs visitors to what is looking best in the garden each day – though it can be selective.

Monday, after being prodded and poked all weekend.' I put my hands guiltily in my pockets.

How do you deal with 182,000 pairs of feet over the space of six months (mid-March to mid-October), especially now the garden is open every day of the week so there's never a day off to recover? Troy tries to save the grass by roping off bits of lawn, two days at a time. The development of the wider estate means that visitors can now explore beyond the garden and, with luck, be less inclined to linger within the walls. Still, the garden is what they've come for, and on a summer Sunday that may mean two and a half thousand people packed into a scant ten acres. 'They've come for the sense of beauty and peace and romance that Vita was so keen on, and you just can't get that with so many people. As soon as you're having to wait to let this or that person pass, or you're worrying where you put your feet, you're no longer involving yourself with the emotional experience.'

Troy likes the gardeners to be visible in the garden – leaving tools around, or standing pots in the border while they mull over where to place them, are habits he actively encourages. He wants visitors to appreciate that it's graft and skill that creates the beauties of Sissinghurst, not some species of ancestral magic.

Troy likes the gardeners to be visible as they go about their work, here clearing up leaves into giant hessian sacks.

The downside is that it's harder to get things done, as the gardeners' work is constantly interrupted. 'Every gardener's a PR man now, whether they like it or not,' comments Troy coolly. He even writes a blog. 'It's not a marketing tool,' he insists. 'We don't need any more visitors. But as a gardener I want to tell stories to add more interest to the visit, so people will get more out of it.' He wants his visitors to understand what they see.

——◆——

Troy was brought up with a keen appreciation of nature. The family lived in west Leeds, and took every opportunity to get out to the Yorkshire Dales. His dad was a twitcher, always out photographing birds, and his uncle was also a keen naturalist. Troy remembers being amazed by the limestone pavements around Malham Cove, the stunted hawthorns and rowans, the plants growing impossibly deep down in the cracks.

'I go to a lot of gardens that I used to visit ten or twenty years ago, and I don't think they are as good as they were. I don't feel that there's the depth of knowledge that the old head gardeners had. Things aren't being passed down as they used to be.'

In 1987, aged sixteen and keen to work outdoors, he left school to work as a trainee gardener at Harewood House. After six months, the head gardener decamped to start his own landscaping business, and Troy went with him. After a stint in France, Troy enrolled at Askham Bryan College in York to study horticulture, which meant spending a year working in a garden. Here he struck gold. He was sent to Bodnant in Snowdonia, a garden that offered both magnificent formal terraces and eighty expansive acres planted with one of the finest woody plant collections in Europe. There's a parallel here: he went to Bodnant as a student gardener in 1990 to return years later as head gardener, and he has done much the same at Sissinghurst, returning to the scene of his first job as a newly qualified gardener.

Troy arrived to work under Sarah Cook, who in turn had been trained by Pamela Schwerdt and Sibylle Kreutzberger. They were both graduates of the famous Waterperry School of Horticulture whose fearsome principal, Miss Beatrix Havergal, is reputed to be the inspiration for Roald Dahl's Miss Trunchbull. 'Sissinghurst was a great place to be in those formative years,' says Troy. 'The standard was so high, the observation, the attention to detail. Sarah had only been here a year or so, so it still ran in the Pam and Sibylle way – I think it set me up to be a decent gardener.'

His next move was to The Courts, a small National Trust garden in Wiltshire, then little known and perhaps a little run-down. His title was 'Gardener in Charge', and Troy was, indeed, in charge of everything: writing the guidebook, ordering the loo rolls, counting the money and then replanning and replanting the garden. It rapidly

Harold was a master of creating intriguing new vistas that propel you onwards through the garden.

gained a reputation for its complex, layered, magnificently textured planting, boosting visitor numbers from nine thousand to thirty thousand in just five years.

'It felt very free: it felt very much my garden. There were great people there who worked very hard, and I really threw myself into it.' It was at The Courts that he developed his photography, going out morning and evening with his camera, a skill that won him the title of RHS Professional Photographer of the Year in 2003. 'It helps you look in a different way and to analyze. It makes you more observant and that really helps the garden.'

That careful scrutiny, that depth of involvement, gave him, he thinks, some of the happiest moments of his life. 'I remember we had an open evening for a sculpture show and we'd worked hard to get the garden spot-on for that, and we just about got there. That's so rare in a garden. We almost achieved, in that one moment, perfection – that's how it felt at the time.'

His next step was less joyous: in 2005 Troy became curator at Hyde Hall, the RHS show garden in Essex. It was a wrong move for him, and he left at the end of the year. The following spring, however, Troy returned to Bodnant, now as head gardener and full of plans to update the garden, to rejuvenate the world-famous botanical collection and bring more visitors in. 'Bodnant was my first garden, so it was always going to be special. I remembered so much of the trees and the water and the smells of the azaleas. I'd always loved the garden, and tried to identify the good and the bad bits and why it was lovely, and – just as here – I could see myself being able to make some improvements ...' Over ten years he masterminded a host of massive projects – major structural improvements such as relining the ponds, putting a tunnel under the road and building a new visitor centre. His children were born and went to the local school. They learned to speak Welsh. There was enough to do at Bodnant to keep Troy busy and engaged for a lifetime. But what

about his children? The job opportunities in rural North Wales were few and far between. And, increasingly, managing a team of twenty, he felt he was becoming remote from the garden.

'I wasn't gardening as often as I should have been, and I was missing the connection with detailed herbaceous planting. Although we did put some in, we didn't have the resources to make it really sing. Increasingly I was coming to understand that this was such a huge project it would never be finished. What I wanted was a vision for five or seven or ten years that could actually be achieved, so you could tick some of it off.' So when the post at Sissinghurst came up, despite his wife's initial reluctance, he applied.

Troy is a very thorough man. 'I read every book that had been written about Sissinghurst, and every word that Vita wrote.' He went to see Sibylle and plumbed her memories. He visited Vita's earlier garden at Long Barn, near Sevenoaks in Kent. 'Then I prepared a document to help me formulate my thoughts: it was all about vision and change.' It was a high-risk strategy: Sissinghurst is widely regarded as the most effulgent jewel in the National Trust's crown, and the Trust might well have taken the view that 'if it ain't broke, don't fix it'. But Troy was in a strong position,

FROM LEFT TO RIGHT *Plant labels are never thrown away: they constitute a record of the many plant combinations that have been tried out over the years. A delivery note to Harold Nicolson from Ralph Cusack of Co. Wicklow, grower and importer of rare bulbs, corms and tubers. One of Harold's planting notebooks, detailing his plans for the Lime Walk. In the fridge where Troy keeps his seeds is a painted seedbox of Vita's, still in everyday use.*

in a garden he didn't need to leave, so he felt he could speak his mind. 'I was pretty honest about where the garden could be better.'

'Don't get me wrong,' he says earnestly. 'I think Sissinghurst has served itself well. It's brought in the numbers, because of Vita and Harold and then their son Nigel talking about their lives; and then also because of the great horticultural techniques that were deployed here. People really responded to that throughout the 1980s and 1990s: so many people copied those techniques and planting styles and plant associations. But I wonder if it's still the right approach now? Other gardens that are freer to do as they please now do some of the things we do here better than us. So perhaps we should be returning to a looser, more fluid, more flexible kind of gardening?'

He can see the framework of the garden crying out for a more spontaneous and ebullient style, more in keeping with Vita's romantic vision. But it's hard — it goes against the grain. He's instinctively orderly — a wiper down of counters and fluffer up of cushions who keeps a clear desk and a tidy mind. 'I like a nice edge and a path clear of weeds, and I have to really go against my nature. Professional gardeners are in general well-organized, tidy people.'

Little by little, smooth lawn is giving way to areas of rough grass, self-seeding is being encouraged, outlines are getting shaggier. He's a firm believer in editing: 'You can usually make a garden better by taking things away.' But what happens when that manky rose turns out to be historically significant, or one especially beloved by Vita? He observes that Vita loved old things that were a bit tattered, like the threadbare cushions in her tower room. But plants don't really do shabby chic; they just look poorly. He has started on a major programme to reintroduce Vita's beloved old roses, for of the 194 varieties growing before 1953, fewer than one hundred remain. Maybe she grew tired of them, or they succumbed to disease, or Pamela or Sarah or Alexis simply found better ones? Troy has made it his business to find out. Then there are areas of the garden that don't work, that have never worked — odd, formless patches here and there. Maybe they need some more radical treatment? He has boldly hacked back the azalea walk. The orchard, he hopes, will take shape over the next twenty years. Which leaves the big one — Sissinghurst's legendary White Garden. Troy is coming round to the view that the time has come to rip it all out and start again.

Dionysus looks out over moat and lawn. The press of visitors is now so great that parts of the lawns have to be roped off in rotation, to give them time to recover.

He's honest enough to admit that the louder the squeals, the more determined he will be to do it. 'This is the first time I've gone to a place and felt really confident. Coming to Sissinghurst aged forty-two, I finally felt I had enough experience, so I would know what to do, even if people didn't like it. I'm trying to make sure, every day, that I think, rather than just garden. Why am I doing this? Does that work or doesn't it? I'm being hypercritical, but it's my job to be. I want Sissinghurst to be here – beautiful, emotional, romantic – in five, twenty, fifty years' time.

'What I want to do over the next few years is to write quite clear recipes – management plans for each garden space – so that if I do get knocked over by a bus, it will be evident, for instance in the White Garden, what we know about the garden, how it should look and what we have to do to achieve that. Somebody may then decide to change all that.' He doesn't mind: gardens need to change, or they atrophy. 'But at least we will have identified what is needed if we're serious about being more pure and authentic to Vita while at the same time respecting the subsequent layers. The challenge is how to do that without alienating people who love it now, how to inject a true sense of beauty and romance, yet still be able to handle nearly two hundred thousand visitors.'

———◦———

Troy would never consider working in a private garden: he likes his work to be seen, known and appreciated by a wider public. Yet sometimes, he confides, he dreams of a garden of his own. A garden with a view, perhaps on a mountainside, with only a small enclosed area for fancy cultivation – a place entirely unconstrained. Perhaps he would teach? He frets that fine gardening skills are not being passed on. Comparing his generation of head gardeners with those he met at his first National Trust conference in 1997, he feels they lack the depth of knowledge of the old guard – the Jimmy Hancocks, Phil Cottons and Mike Snowdons (of Powis, Cliveden and Rowallane Garden respectively) – men with whole lifetimes of experience. He wants to set up training schemes at Sissinghurst, and is already creating links with local schools and colleges.

But all that comes second to the long process of rethinking, replanting and renewal he sees ahead. He reads a few pages of Vita's columns every day, tries to see what she saw, to capture her joy in the garden she was making. He'll know he has succeeded when he can imagine her striding, all top-boots and pearls, through a garden she could once more acknowledge as her own.

A quiet spot away from the horticultural fireworks.

SPACE FOR THOUGHT

LUCILLE SAVIN
Merton College, Oxford

'I like to think the students might remember Merton,
when the time comes, and do better.'

ACCORDING TO TRADITION, Oxbridge college servants must be elderly, portly, irredeemably world-weary and acid of tongue. So the Pre-Raphaelite beauty in green overalls flitting between the trees in the Merton College garden rather subverts the stereotype — not least since she is sweet of voice and sunny of disposition. Every passing student calls out a greeting, which she acknowledges with a cheery wave of her secateurs. Some stop for a chat. She chats but doesn't stop. Merton College, Oxford, appointed its first female warden in 1994. A female head gardener — arguably the more significant position to the everyday lives of the students — took another eight years.

Lucille Savin is possessed of a radiant calm and positive energy of a kind that makes ordinary mortals feel a tad underpowered. Yet there are moments when even the most stalwart heart must sink. This is one of them: Lucille watches silently, hands stuffed deep in her pockets, as half a dozen men with mallets lay into her precious garden.

'It will recover,' she says brightly. 'We're all used to events in the garden.' It's just that this is no run-of-the-mill garden party. The occasion is a lavish ball to mark the 750th anniversary of the college. There's a dodgem track going up in Front Quad, and a coconut shy on the Sundial Lawn, and now the velvet turf of the Fellows' Garden is disappearing under a small village of outsize marquees. Cables are hurled carelessly across her carefully nurtured herbaceous borders; car-sized arc lights are plonked willy-nilly. 'It will all be fine,' insists Lucille. 'And it *is* rather exciting.' She is not a woman given to panic.

'You have to remember it's not my garden,' she says, with unreasonable reasonableness. 'It's Merton's garden, and it must serve their purposes.' Those purposes may be outdoor plays (there's one every summer), or croquet, or parties, or wedding receptions, or less formal celebrations such as post-exam 'trashings', when students merrily douse each other in flour, champagne, ketchup and baked beans. 'They're always very good about clearing up the mess,' she says forgivingly.

Then there are regular visits from film crews, especially for the Oxford-based detective series *Morse*, *Lewis* and *Endeavour*. The corpse count is high. Once she was asked to mock up a pond into which a victim might be pushed from an upstairs window. There is also, of course, a graveyard.

But the principal aim of the garden, to Lucille's mind, is to provide a space of calm and quiet and mental refreshment. Merton has long been regarded as one of Oxford's brainiest colleges, and even though Lucille has found it an unusually friendly and supportive one, the terms are short, the workload enormous, the pressure relentless, and student stress can reach stratospheric proportions. Spending time quietly in the garden, she observes, helps many students regain some kind of balance.

She often looks up to find someone palely loitering, silently watching her work. Mostly, they haven't a clue what she's doing: they just find the purposeful activity in some way soothing. She hopes that in some strange, osmotic way, gardening is rubbing off. 'I hope that later in their lives it will inspire them to think what's achievable. So often now, people don't have any aspiration for a garden at all. All around where I live are these awful little beaches of gravel, so miserable and uninspiring. I like to think the students might remember Merton, when the time comes, and do better.'

———•◦•———

Merton is Oxford's oldest and, for many, most beautiful college, founded in 1264 by Walter de Merton, sometime Chancellor of England and later Bishop of Rochester. Mob Quad, the oldest quadrangle in the university, was begun around 1288, and the library there is the oldest continuously functioning university library in the world. Every stone is steeped in history; every corner has some significance. Here, in the thirteenth-century chapel (remodelled in the nineteenth century by William Butterfield and Sir Gilbert Scott), is a screen by Sir Christopher Wren. There, half hidden among wild flowers, is a memorial to Andrew 'Sandy' Irvine, undergraduate of the college, who perished with George Mallory near the summit of Everest, aged just twenty-two. The walls that lap the college were once the city walls, and the raised

Nearly every wall at Merton is clothed in climbers, and keeping them in check to allow the students some light is one of the less rewarding garden occupations.

The Grove adjoining the thirteenth-century college chapel is managed as a wildflower meadow, lovely in spring with bulbs and blossom, but carefully paced to keep going well into summer.

walk alongside them part of the fortifications when Oxford was a Royalist stronghold during the English Civil War. There, at one end, is a hexagonal stone table where Merton's Professor of English Language and Literature, one J. R. R. Tolkien, would sit looking out over Christ Church Meadow, no doubt dreaming of hobbits. This same table is said to have inspired the one on which the lion Aslan is slain in the Narnia books of his friend C. S. Lewis (though it's scarcely large enough to hold a cat). No fewer than four Nobel laureates have trod these paths.

So the weight of tradition is palpable: an awe-inspiring sense of all the men (exclusively men until 1980) who have savoured these views and walked these lawns and maybe stretched out in the shade of some ancient tree and thought some great thought that changed the world. But here is the great dichotomy of a place like Merton: the whole point of it is to think afresh, to dare to articulate something entirely new. It is here that William Harvey discovered the circulation of the blood; that mathematician Andrew Wiles, after three hundred and fifty years, finally solved

LEFT Salvia guarantica, Echium pininiana, Romneya coulteri *and* Mandevilla suaveolens, *normally considered a conservatory plant, thrive in the shelter of the Meadow Walk.* RIGHT *Fruitily scented* Salvia macrophylla *and* Echium pininiana *under a curtain of* Solanum crispum.

Fermat's Last Theorem; that T. S. Eliot reinvented twentieth-century poetry. And it is just that stirring sense of the old and the new intertwined that is Lucille's inspiration in the garden. On the one hand, she finds a deep and settled contentment in the knowledge that this piece of land has been a sanctuary for the college fellows since the thirteenth century. On the other, she cultivates a sense of adventure: this is no safe, traditionalist garden, but brimming with new plants, new experiments, new ideas.

At the eastern end of the garden, the once gloomy Grove has been transformed into a magical wildflower meadow where the usual campions and cow parsleys are augmented by blood-red anemones, pyramid orchids and elecampane. It's an intimate, wild, poetic space that makes a fine contrast with the austere grass square of Fellows' Quad or the cobbled formality of Front Quad.

Encouraged by the shelter of ancient walls (although some aren't nearly so venerable as they appear), Lucille has introduced a tumult of half-hardy colour. Fragrant paperwhite narcissi, more usually forced indoors, start off the show in spring,

Bold scarlet Campsis × tagliabuana *'Madame Galen' flowers so vigorously that every February it must be cut right back to its skeletal frame.*

followed by great papery blooms of romneya, a mass of jewel-coloured salvias, scarlet cannas and purple hibiscus. Echiums lean drunkenly over the wall towards Christ Church Meadow. A huge mandevilla, usually considered a conservatory plant, shins carelessly up a drainpipe. *Campsis × tagliabuana* 'Madame Galen', dripping waxy bells of fire-engine red, grows so vigorously it must be ruthlessly hacked back every February. More colour erupts in enormous containers dotted throughout the quads. They are coming into their own just as the students leave for the summer, but the conference guests enjoy them, and they are still looking good in October, when the academic year begins. 'We like to give a good first impression to new students,' says Lucille, 'and also to reassure the parents dropping them off that Merton's a nice place to be.'

Indeed, Lucille has made those freshers a special welcome. In the bland 1940s quad where they are billeted, she has torn out a shabby rose garden and replaced it with an exotic foliage display dominated by a vast tetrapanax, each leaf the size of an umbrella. It survives without the least pampering, even when specimens just across the road in the botanic garden are cut to the ground by frost.

*The admin block is the unlikely setting for a fabulous subtropical garden, featuring angel's trumpets (*Brugmansia suaveolens), bananas *(*Musa basjoo), *Tetrapanax papyrifer* 'Rex' *and* Echium pininiana *amidst a jungle of ferns and bamboos.*

Even more adventurous is the Warden's Garden that adjoins it. A blank square of lawn just three years ago, it is now a riotous jungle garden, a joyous explosion of outsize leaves and great gaudy blooms — bananas and cannas and more tetrapanax, ginger lilies and arums of improbably huge proportions (*Zantedeschia* 'White Giant' lives extravagantly up to its name), with puddles of vivid annuals round their feet. The warden and his wife, who had spent several happy years in the Caribbean, had requested a garden with 'a bit more zing'.

'In Caribbean gardens pink, yellow, orange, anything — all look great together, because they get so much light, whereas in our light levels the combinations jar or look clashing. But in here we do whatever we like, Christopher Lloyd-style.' Lucille beams delightedly.

Lucille used bamboos and the giant reed *Arundo donax* to create instant height and enclosure but the fan palms (*Trachycarpus fortunei*) and bananas (*Musa basjoo*) have shot up so quickly, the reeds are almost redundant. While a series of cold winters slowed the orange ginger lily *Hedychium densiflorum* 'Assam Orange', its relative *Hedychium forrestii* has romped away unaffected, and nicotiana, intended as an annual, often survives to flower a second year.

Bolder still are the two adjoining gardens Lucille has created across the road, around new quarters for Merton's office staff. Here the exuberance of massed exotics contrasts effectively with a minimalist structure of pale new stone. Rampant climbers soften the rather shed-like backdrop of a real tennis court (one of the oldest in the land). And dense, richly textured foliage – the lush greens shot through with the odd dash of purple – sets off the quiet formality of an angular pool to create an atmosphere that is simultaneously wildly rich and deeply tranquil. Of all her achievements at Merton – the massive herbaceous borders, a new fruit garden, the careful placing of tree and leaf against honeyed stone – this is perhaps her proudest.

'You know you have a moment in your life where you think, yes, I can do this, rather than feeling insecure. I realized, yes, Lucille, you're really doing it, this is you.'

'I'd not really done much garden design before, but you know you have a moment in your life where you think, yes, I can do this, rather than feeling insecure. I realized, yes, Lucille, you're really doing it, this is *you*. That was an important eye-opener for me.'

The teenage Lucille Savin didn't want to be a teacher or a nurse or a policewoman. In truth, she had no clue what she wanted to do with her life. But she liked pottering around in the garden, and proposing to study horticulture was enough to get teachers and parents off her back. By the end of her degree course at Writtle College she was hooked, and genuinely astonished when most of her classmates elected not to stay in horticulture. Lucille had lined up a job at Oxford University Parks and couldn't wait to get started.

By twenty-three, Lucille was parks foreman, managing an all-male workforce twice or three times her own age. 'Luckily we hit it off. Sometimes they'd know a better way of doing things, and sometimes I would. So between us, it worked really well. I think they secretly quite liked having a woman looking after them.'

After seven happy but impecunious years, Lucille moved to the Cotswolds to work for Carole Bamford at Daylesford, home of the Daylesford Organic empire. As well as a highly ornamental productive garden, there were woodland and wildflower areas, formal terraces and a constant demand for plant material for decorating the house. There was all the excitement of a developing a garden, with dozens of trees

Lucille is very conscious of the centuries of history that give Merton its potent atmosphere. At the same time, these have been 750 years of intellectual questing and innovation, and she feels the garden should embody that too.

and thousands of bulbs going in each year. 'The contrast couldn't have been more complete — not so much learning to garden organically as moving to an environment where money was no object,' says Lucille. 'If you wanted a mature tree, you just JCB'd it in. It was a fabulous garden, but Daylesford gardening was all about bulk-buying ready-grown plants. There wasn't so much anticipation. Here, when I want something, I have to nurture it from small.'

She returned to Oxford in 2002 to take up the post at Merton. It is a wealthy college, so while it could hardly compete with Daylesford, you might expect the garden budget to be generous. Lucille winces ever so slightly. 'The problem is that as a department we are spenders, rather than bringing in income. We know the garden is greatly valued by the students and also, increasingly, by conference guests. But there's always money going out, and it's not easy to quantify the value we give to the college.'

'Head gardener is a term that, in Oxford at least, seems to be losing its value. More and more colleges now employ "garden managers". It's a shame, because the head gardener role has so much history, and embodies hands-on skills as well as managerial ones, whereas most managers can only manage.'

Compared with a National Trust gardener, she concedes, she doesn't do badly. She feels fortunate to have three full-time staff to care for the six and a half acres of the college site, plus extensive student accommodation, with gardens dotted across the town. She also has a free hand. She reports to a Garden Master, a Fellow appointed by the college to oversee the garden but who has no real involvement with the day to day management. When major decisions have to be made — such as felling the diseased tree that gave its name to the Chestnut Lawn and deciding on a replacement — a committee of fellows gets involved. Sometimes there are bigger issues, and then she needs to find the confidence to speak up.

'All the fellows are used to public speaking; they're very confident in their fields of work and they all know each other. And there you are, this little grubby head gardener, having to champion the garden. Sometimes you have to stick up for it, like persuading a building committee to do something differently, in a way that would be less detrimental to the garden. They might not want to hear it, but it's important that it should be said.'

If it takes some guts to argue against some of the biggest brains on the planet, she's glad at least to have the opportunity. Many of the colleges — even those with important historic gardens like New College — don't have their own gardeners any more, but employ contractors. Then there's no one to defend the garden's interest. Often, the contractor of choice is the University Parks service; indeed, Lucille worked in many of the colleges during her parks days. But it's a totally different way of gardening, she finds: one that inhibits the development of a strong sense of connection with the garden and the people who use it. And the worst of it is, it's increasingly de-skilled.

'"Head gardener" is a term that, in Oxford at least, seems to be losing its value,' she says. 'More and more colleges now employ "garden managers". It's a shame, because the head gardener role has so much history, and embodies hands-on skills as well as managerial ones, whereas most managers can only manage. As a parks foreman I spent seven years in a purely supervisory role: it's so much more rewarding to be hands-on again.'

Ask any Mertonian, past or present, where their sense of belonging resides and the garden is always near the top of the list. Hands in the soil, day in, day out, Lucille and her team are crucial members of the Merton family. Gardens in Oxford have always been vulnerable: colleges like Oriel and All Souls built over most of their gardens centuries ago. Keeping Merton's garden relevant and loved, she also keeps it safe: a timeless haven of seclusion and peace that continues to sustain successive generations of scholars.

Lucille hopes that when the students leave, some residual delight in gardening will have rubbed off on them.

WHAT'S THE BIG IDEA?

ALISTAIR CLARK
Garden of Cosmic Speculation, Dumfries

'This is landscape design at its best and simplest —
water, lines and grass — nothing else.'

'**T**HIS IS THE THIRTEEN BILLION** years from the onset of the universe to the present day, so you're starting away down there with protons, neutrons, gravity, matter, light — you see light in the blue? And then there is the supernova break-up — see the bit with the red stones? And then you come across to the various orbits of the planets, and on to reproduction, "Life Eat Life", photosynthesis and symbiosis; the ammonite extinctions at 505, 245, 214 and 65 million years ago, so each time the tank fills the ammonites are almost wiped out and then they recuperate and build up again. This is the brain here, in the red; this is man; that over there is religion; and there's woman and puberty over that side — you can just about see woman underneath. This is modernity here . . . it's coming up to the present time here, and over here is the future.'

Alistair Clark has it all off pat, and rattles it off with the velocity and dash of a Gilbert and Sullivan patter song. Over the years, he has come to have more than a passing acquaintance with cosmology, astrophysics and molecular biology.

He is standing now in the Garden of Cosmic Speculation at Portrack House near Dumfries, at the summit of the Universe Cascade, a white concrete water-staircase conceived by his boss, Charles Jencks, but realized by Alistair, that purports to tell the story of cosmic evolution from the dawn of time to the present day and beyond.

For the last twenty years, he has travelled the world making astonishing pieces of land art with similarly grandiose themes — in Dublin and Milan, in India, Korea and the United States — and is currently engaged in interpreting the multiverse in water,

earth and sandstone just up the road at Crawick. It is not the trajectory he would have predicted for the shy dairyman's lad who started out sweeping out the glasshouses at the age of thirteen, and who for years had no more world-shaking ambitions than to breed handsome hybrid begonias.

In those days, these forty peaceable acres beside the River Nith were untroubled by cosmic speculations. Portrack, then, was a proper, old-fashioned Scottish estate garden. The owner, Sir John Keswick, previously head of the trading dynasty Jardine Matheson, loved shooting, fishing and showy rhododendrons. He was friends with the plant-hunting Coxes at Glendoick, and enjoyed a regular annual shipment of new specimens from Hilliers and Sunningdale nurseries. His wife, Clare, liked to fill the house with flowers: sweet peas, lilies, roses (they grew over one hundred hybrid teas for cutting), and pots of lilies, gloxinias and carnations. 'When they weren't in residence here,' recalls Alistair, 'I'd be off to the station every second Monday, with twenty dozen carnations to send to their place in London.'

Looking down the Universe Cascade, a monumental water staircase that gives a symbolic account of the evolution of the cosmos, described in twenty-six stages or 'jumps'.

The Keswicks were proud of their garden. 'When Sir John and Lady Keswick were alive, they'd often have three lots of visitors a day — one before lunch, one in the afternoon and one for dinner — and they never tired of walking them around the garden. There were more than one hundred and fifty genus of plants in the greenhouses then — genus, not species or cultivars. There were over one hundred fuchsias, three hundred pots of perpetual flowering carnations. I went on to specialize in hybrid begonias, growing five hundred named varieties and seven hundred seedlings a year.' The fruit and vegetables were no less impressive. 'We grew our own nectarines, peaches and grapes, as well as strawberries, raspberries and currants,' says Alistair. 'We grew every vegetable you could name, packing three or four crops into every inch of ground. In those days, people would flock to the open days just to see the vegetables and the greenhouses. These days, no one much goes there any more.'

Shortly after his fifteenth birthday, Alistair started work full-time as an apprentice gardener. He didn't want to. He wanted to stay on at school and become a maths teacher. But he was one of eight children, and money was tight.

'My mum was boss in the house, and because all my brothers and sisters had left school — even though none of them had wanted to stay on — she said I had to, too. But that's history. She knew the head gardener, and got me the job here.'

Sandy Niven might not have had much in the way of formal training, but he was a top-notch practical gardener and an excellent teacher for the young Alistair. 'We never fed any of our plants, yet he could grow onions twenty-two inches in diameter. It was him who started me off on begonias. He was an old bugger and he was hard, but in the long run he did me a lot of good.

'He was a bit of a lad,' remembers Alistair with a grin. 'If he wasn't away fishing, he was away golfing, and if he wasn't away golfing, he was away with the women.' He had an excellent work ethic as far as his workers were concerned, however. 'Even in the winter, when it was dark at half past three, we never got away early — he'd have us in the saw-shed cutting up logs, or making articles for the greenhouse or stakes for the garden. He'd say: "Ah, it must be getting near five o'clock," and it would be half past six. But you couldn't complain. "If you're not happy," he'd say, "ye can get off down the road."'

Alistair remembers many hours spent digging out the bottoms of trenches, while Mr Niven dug out the tops. 'If he caught up with me, he'd say, "Get a move on boy or you'll get your arse kicked!" It was the same with cutting hedges with the shears — I'd take the bottom half of the hedge and he'd take the top and I couldn't stop unless he did. I had the best of it, because I was young and strong and he needed me to cover for him and get the work done, but there were a couple of men in their sixties, and there were days I would catch them crying. Yet those old boys could cut a hedge with a hedging knife, and never a leaf out of place.'

The hours were long: forty-eight hours a week in summer and forty-three in winter, with only two weeks' holiday and no weekends off. Every Saturday morning Alistair would find himself harvesting vegetables for the house before being despatched to scrub the greenhouse floor and rake the gravel at the front door.

'There were no power tools then. The only machine in the place was a 26-inch cylinder mower,' recalls Alistair. 'I would walk seven and a half miles to cut the lawns.' The banks were still cut with sheep shears, and the long grass with scythes. 'I'd make twenty-two birch brushes a year to sweep the leaves from the lawn which we'd then rot down for leaf mould and mix our own compost. We were completely self-sufficient. We made turf-stacks, layering the turves with lime and farmyard manure. We would collect dried cowpats in the winter, riddle them and add them to the potting compost — we never fed anything in the growing season, and the plants were second to none. We would get gravel out of the river and riddle that too, saving the sharp sand for compost and spreading the gravel around the house. And every year we were stripping the greenhouses, repainting and reglazing them, paving, cobbling, putting in edging, fencing, drystone walling – so when Charles came along it was just an extension of that.'

———⋈———

It was towards the end of the 1980s that Charles Jencks began his landscape experiments at Portrack. By this time Alistair had been head gardener for over a decade. He had built a reputation as one of the top begonia hybridizers in the land and he was very much master of his own domain, enjoying an excellent relationship with the Keswicks and their daughter, Maggie. Alistair and Maggie were much of an age, and were the best of friends. Although Maggie had spent much of her childhood in London, China and Hong Kong, she and Alistair had, to a certain extent, grown up together at Portrack, and Alistair had the deepest respect for her both as a person and as a knowledgeable plantswoman. She was also an authority on Chinese gardens, describing them as 'cosmic diagrams, revealing a profound and ancient view of the world, and of man's place in it'. So when she married Charles Jencks, the American architect, theoretician and self-styled inventor of postmodernism, she already had a broader view of what a garden could be than simply a bountiful provider of fruit and flowers. A garden, she knew, could tell stories, and express the deepest truths of human existence.

So whose idea was a Garden of Cosmic Speculation? Alistair can't be sure. 'Maggie wanted Charles to get interested, so she started developing the garden from the late 1980s. And it worked – he *did* get interested.' Their plan was to dig out a boggy area at the lowest point in the garden to make a swimming lake for their children, John and Lily. The spoil, they decided, would be built up into mounts or ramparts, calling in the shapes of the distant hills. For Maggie, it was natural that these should represent the 'land-dragons' on the horizon. (If you live in Wales or West Dorset, you will perfectly understand the Chinese concept of the living landscape, where hills are the bones of the earth, or dragons sleeping under a blanket of soil.) But these sculptural forms could express, equally well, the scientific and cosmological concepts that Charles was exploring in his work. Most excitingly, he proposed a new geometry of fractals, of forms based on curves and waves and the self-similarity apparent in nature, to displace the Euclidean geometry that underlies the Western garden. And so evolved the Snail Mound and the Snake Mound, sinuous green landforms curling around serene sheets of water. With their paths that force you to walk up to go down, and down to go up, they embody a complex of meanings ranging from the pilgrim's journey and redemption to the structure of DNA.

Ask Alistair nicely, and he'll lead you patiently through every reference – the double staircase at Chambord that allows two people to pass without meeting, Tatlin's Tower, Marxist dialectic, the structure of the double helix . . . 'But to me it doesn't matter what it signifies. You can tell anyone anything: if you're convincing they'll believe it. To me,' and his tone is almost reverent, 'this has no need of scientific explanation. This is landscape design at its best and simplest – water, lines and grass – nothing else.'

After a day with Alistair Clark, you understand exactly why the Scots have conquered the planet, furnishing the most resolute explorers, the most inventive engineers, covering continents in railways and changing the world in all manner of ingenious ways from the steam engine to Dolly the sheep. At seventy, Alistair is as strong and fit as a man half his age. (Indeed, both he and his wife of fifty years look so astonishingly youthful that if they lived in Los Angeles you'd suspect them of having had 'work'.) He is clearly a man who will turn his hand to anything and relish the challenge. So while another head gardener might have retreated, muttering, to the greenhouse, Alistair set his mind to how to sculpt the land. The new project was very much a joint effort. While Maggie worked on the shape of the lakes, trying out her ideas on Alistair (who claims credit for the central causeway), Charles drew up the landforms, which Alistair must somehow conjure, crisp and pristine, from the swampy ground. There were no technical drawings. 'For the Snail Mound, Charles gave me a cement model and I mapped out the base area with sawdust. There was no measuring with rules or lines – it was all done by eye.'

The Snail Mound, a conical hill over 15 metres high, was built on a core of gravel dug from the upper part of the garden. This was topped with a deep (80 cm) blanket of topsoil sufficient to carve out its spiralling surface. To shape the landform, Alistair, aided by his three gardeners, started at the top, digging out the lines by hand, as and when they could between their other garden duties. Lady Keswick was still in residence, and watching with apprehension as these curious new forms took shape in her garden. 'Once we had the lines down halfway, contractors could continue with JCBs, but in those days there were no swivel buckets, so there was a limit to what machines could do.' They finished the Snail Mound in 1993, and moved on to the Snake Mound, a loosely S-shaped rampart some 120 metres long. This was harder to shape, Alistair recalls, as they had run out of gravel and were working with sludge from the lakes. Good drainage and soil compaction were key if the forms were to hold without slipping. 'In October it was so wet that we had to abandon the south side and couldn't restart till 1995. We didn't want to damage what we'd already done, so we were carrying buckets of topsoil up ladders by hand and foot-tramping. So Maggie never saw the last 30 or 40 metres of the Snake, or the complete panorama with the lake.'

PAGES 144–145 *The Snail Mount and Double Helix landforms.*

Maggie had been diagnosed with breast cancer in 1989, which recurred in 1993. Her experience at that time led her to found her eponymous charity, building Maggie's Centres to support cancer patients and their families (there are now seventeen worldwide). As Alistair tells her story, his indignation burns as fresh as ever.

'Maggie had a mastectomy in 1989, then took unwell again in 1993. She went up to Edinburgh and they said, "Do you want the bad news? You've got three months to live." And then, having been told that, she was made to wait in a corridor on one of those plastic chairs, with nurses going by saying: "Hello dearie, how are you today? Isn't it a nice day?" without realizing what's just happened. Maggie thought this was terrible, so she spent the rest of her time setting up a new cancer unit in Edinburgh where you can learn about your illness and get help to manage it, for she was a great believer in managing her own illness. She said then, "It's not so much the cancer that kills you as the thought of having it." All the time she was ill she was working on her plans, and the first centre opened the year after she died.'

'America would have been a poor show had it not been for the Scotch.'

ANDREW CARNEGIE

For two years, though, Maggie was well, out with Alistair in the rain stamping down the turf on the mounds, and brimming over with plans for the garden. She had an undulating drystone 'Dragon Wall' built alongside a new kitchen garden, which she had conceived as a Tartan Garden with a little summer house in each of its six segments. This would evolve, after her death, into the DNA or Physics Garden, representing each of the five senses (plus a sixth — woman's intuition) and crammed with esoteric sculpture, riddles and word games.

Maggie's death hit Alistair hard. He knew she was going to die, he says, the day in July 1995 that she arrived from London and walked around the garden with him, arm in arm, issuing a sheaf of instructions on what must be done in the winter — shrubs to be planted, trees to be felled. 'She'd never ever given me notes before,' recalls Alistair. 'That was a Tuesday. The following Saturday, she was dead.'

It is fair to say that, in the intervening years, Alistair has guarded Portrack as a kind of shrine to Maggie. The Garden of Cosmic Speculation, which began with lighthearted wordplay (the tennis court, for instance, was designated the Garden of the Sense of Fair Play), has taken on its own momentum, sprouting more and more features — some simply beautiful (as in the waveforms that animate the garden, the sweeping ha-ha and curling red Chinese bridges), others eccentric or didactic.

Alistair's favourite part of the garden, however, remains more or less untouched — a quiet, wild area of wood and stream, where ferns and rhododendrons scramble over the ruins of a thirteenth-century castle. Here, at the water's edge, stands a statue of Maggie: beautiful, full-breasted, veiled in ferns. On the other side of the copse

This portrait bust of Alistair, created by Charles Jencks's sister Penelope, was commissioned by Jencks to mark fifty years of loyal service. So there's never a moment when Alistair hasn't got his eye on the garden.

is another statue, looking out in the opposite direction. It is a bust of Alistair, back to back with Maggie, placed in the garden to mark fifty years of dedicated service.

'We all thought when Maggie died we wouldn't see much of Charlie, because he's a lecturer in California.' Alistair couldn't have been more wrong. The Portrack landforms were featured on TV, and Jencks was invited to create a similar feature at the Scottish National Gallery of Modern Art in Edinburgh in 2000. Alistair went along too. This would be the first of many such projects, working first with Charles and later with Charles and Maggie's daughter, Lily, who is also a landscape architect.

'The Edinburgh waveform is where Charles struck lucky,' says Alistair. 'It brought him commissions from all over the world. Every one he does has a different theme: the one at Jupiter Artland, Edinburgh, is all about cell division; the one near Newcastle, at Northumberlandia, is all about parts of a lady; the one at Crawick is all about the different galaxies. The only one I've not been to is Cern in Switzerland, but all the others I've been very much involved in and have thoroughly enjoyed.'

Most gardens are designed on a Euclidean geometry of circles, rectangles and straight lines; but this instead adopts the new fractal geometry of waves and twists — right down to the fences, the ha-ha and this metalwork gate.

In all his travels, he's noticed a pattern. 'I find people can get their levels right now (I can remember going over to Milan and the levels were spot on and I thought, "At last!"), but no one can get a continuous curve – it's either a fast curve or a slow curve or it's got a kink in it; I can't get anyone to do that right, and I don't know why that is. In Edinburgh they were using theodolites and all manner of gadgets, but you still have to satisfy the eye. Look at it from above, I said, and from below, from the east and from the west. Look at it every time you go down for your lunch or your tea or last thing at night. You need your base area marked out, but after that, you must trust in your eye, because that's how other people will see it.' 'Sweet' is the word he uses for it – making patterns of sweet curves.

Meanwhile, as the Garden of Cosmic Speculation gathered pace, Alistair's range of skills was put to the test: laying out a Quark Walk of painted wooden poles, cutting up slices of concrete to build a Forces of Matter seat based on the Higgs boson particle, constructing a terrace in AstroTurf and gravel to simulate a black hole, and a Symmetry Break in crisply edged strips of grass. For over a year he laboured on the Universe Cascade, mocking up various designs for the steps in concrete, working out how to get the water to flow and how to balance enormous Chinese rocks safely on the precarious slope. The position of each is now larded with symbolism, but the truth is, the determining factor was mechanical failure. The building of a new viaduct adjoining the garden led to the creation of a Railway Garden with 'carriages' on the skyline bearing quotations from 'Scottish Worthies', as Alistair calls them. In 2008 he started work on a Birchbone Garden, featuring lengths of rubber tubing, assorted skeletons and a fossilized toad. His metamorphosis was complete, he reflected: instead of propagating plants he was planting bones.

As fast as one feature was complete it was on to the next. This left Alistair with two major headaches: first, that manpower devoted to feature-building was diverted from the garden, and then that all these new features required a high level of maintenance. Bridges, steps and totem poles need annual repainting, birch trunks need scrubbing; aluminium sculptures need hosing down; above all, it's a never-ending task to keep acres of white concrete from turning green and slimy, and grassy banks neat and crisp.

'It's absolute murder, keeping on top of the work,' sighs Alistair, not least since getting two consecutive dry days is a rarity. 'In south-west Scotland, you'll get algae on glass, never mind on concrete. Charles doesn't appreciate that it's the maintenance that makes it: it's got to be pristine to work. He'll say, never mind the grass, let it grow. But what about the lines? There's no point having a landform unless you're going to keep it well.'

It takes a man with a Flymo half a day to cut the Snail Mound, plus two hours with strimmer to cut the angles. The Snake requires three hours with a robot, then half a day with the Flymo and another half with a strimmer. It's hard to think of a more unforgiving garden feature – any weed or dip or bald patch stands out like a sore thumb. Then the lakes must be kept crystal clear and their edges clean and sharp – but before they can be strimmed, the gardeners must wait till the wind is blowing, then scoop out every blade of grass from the side with nets.

'If the time-motion people came here, they'd tell you you need ten or eleven men,' sniffs Alistair. With only four, it's the horticulture that suffers. So much of the work of gardening is invisible to the uninitiated.

'Charles is a clever, clever man, there's no disputing that. But he doesn't know the first thing about horticulture. He didn't when he first came to Portrack and I don't think he does yet.

'Charles will write down all these instructions and want me to do this or that, and doesn't understand that in a garden you have to do the most important job first. So in the nicest possible way, he's a little bit exasperating. Then he'll say, didn't you read my notes? And I'll say, "No, I left them in my pocket and my wife washed my shirt . . ."'

Absolute beauty, reflects Alistair, requires no footnotes. This he considers landscape at its best and simplest. But to maintain it with the crispness he would like is an uphill struggle.

You can imagine the battles — two clever, articulate, stubborn men not given to self-doubt, constantly locking horns. It's fire and granite — the elegant, erudite, hyperactive American pitted against the intransigent Scot.

Alistair likes a good grumble, but he's his own worst enemy. On the site of the former tennis court lies a pile of what can only be described as junk — rusty wheelbarrows, railway-line debris, old girders, bits of pipe. Yet Alistair, largely unprompted, is plotting a Water and Rust Garden, with complicated chutes and rills, and clearly can't wait to get his teeth into a bit of complex water engineering. He's just a boy with the biggest Meccano set in Scotland.

✦

In 2014, Charles and Maggie's son, John, took on responsibility for Portrack. His first act was to beg Alistair not to retire, but to stay in post for a further four years. His plan for Portrack is to put an end to further feature-making, and to concentrate instead on its former glories — flowers, vegetables and fruit.

Alistair's delight is plain to see: he can't wait to get back to proper gardening again, getting the long-neglected greenhouses back up to speed, planting up the kitchen garden that has largely lain fallow, renovating and replanting in Lady Keswick's shrub garden. 'He'll no get rid of his dad's work, because it's nice. But it will be good to get back to a proper garden routine. For years now, if you were caught in the greenhouse or the veg garden by Charles, he'd be angry, but tell him you'd been pouring concrete all day, and he'd be happy as Larry.'

'It's tidiness that makes the place, now we're not growing flowers.'

Obviously, there are hard decisions to be made. The sculptures in the DNA garden, for example, are starting to decay, and they must decide whether, and how, to preserve them. Then the bridges need repair, and the Birchbone Garden could do with better drainage. It's a big investment to keep it all going, and the truth is, if some of this busy-ness were lost, it would be no loss to the garden. For throughout Portrack, it is the simplest effects that are the most telling: the beautiful mounds; the clean line of poplars in the railway garden; some well-considered, faintly oriental planting round the lake. And in so far as Jencks has embraced eighteenth-century practices of manipulating perceptions through structures, naming and inscription, he might see himself as part of a noble tradition in following the fate of The Leasowes, the most influential garden of its day, but which endured for only thirty years.

'Everything that Charles has done at Portrack enhances the place,' is Alistair's final verdict. He's especially pleased with the Railway Garden, which gives the site room to breathe; and he'll steal off on a moonlit night to stand on the bridge and enjoy the poplars reflected in the lake – poplars he planted himself in the late 1950s. The suggestion that he has had a hand in creating one of the more significant gardens of the late twentieth century raises no more than a wry smile. 'I've never looked at it that way. It's a nice place for people to come, but whatever you see in it, there's tons and tons and tons more gardens that are equally as appealing. This one is fortunate to be in the media, and to have a certain following. But to me it's just a job.'

If Alistair has any regrets, it is that perhaps he could have made more of a name for himself had he worked for himself. 'I did think at one time, after working for Maggie in her garden in America, that my golly, I could have a good life out there, running my own business,' he says. 'So when I came back I was unsettled for a while. But I'd been at Portrack thirty years by then and I really liked the Keswicks, so I thought, the heck with it all, I'll just stick here. It's not been a bad life. I've seen the world, and I've been able to do many different jobs. It's been diverse.

'I've never been one to work a thirty-seven-hour week. If something needs to be completed, you're better to go out and do it before it gets too far down the road

Discreet steps allow the gardeners to negotiate a wave-form ha-ha that encloses the upper terraces.

of no return. I think if you're a head gardener, you've got to do that: you can't work to a timetable. But don't get me wrong, I'm not one-eyed where the garden is concerned; I've many other interests as well. I play snooker and squash; I played football till I was fifty-four, and only stopped when I started digging for bottles.'

Collecting bottles (and other discarded ceramics) is Alistair's passion, and there is a room in his house devoted to his treasures — hundreds, nay thousands, of delicate finds arranged in tiers on a snooker table and ranged along the walls. There are chunky stone bottles for whisky and stout and ginger beer, dainty painted pot lids for hand cream or sweeties, faintly spooky fat-cheeked doll's faces and tiny, twinkly medicine bottles. There is cherry-flavoured tooth powder and complexion-enhancing soap and an ointment of 'genuine Russian bear's grease for increasing the growth of hair'. Every one is a miracle of survival.

'The great thing about hunting for bottles is the ecstasy and the despondency you can experience in a split second — you find a pot lid and it's always blank-side up, and for that brief moment all the things that it might be flash through your mind . . . Then if you turn it over and it's blank, you're so cast down. It's like

Alistair's hobby is digging for bottles, and he travels all over Scotland in search of new finds.

fishing: if you go out expecting to find something you'll be disappointed. You can go out on a day like this [it is hurling it down], digging for twelve hours and get nothing, and think, "Why the heck am I doing this?" But next time you've some time off, you're at it again . . .

'Some days I think I should retire. I would hate to work on, and then within six months not be fit enough to do the things I want to do. That happens to a lot of people. I'd like to travel the world for six months, then dig for bottles the other six. I'd like to walk the Inca Trail. But then again I'll think to myself, "I'm still quite fit, why should I give up my work?"'

When he does finally retire, he announces, he intends to write a book about his curious life as a gardener, engineer, metalworker, stonemason, cosmological interpreter and architectural dogsbody. 'I've kept a diary of my work here every day since 1961. I have every scribble, every scrap of paper since I've been at Portrack. So even if the garden disappears, what we did here will be known.'

Garden Museum, take note. The Alistair Clark Archive will be treasure.

MENDING WHAT
IS BROKEN

CAROL SALES
Headley Court, Surrey

'Horticulture has to be useful, practical, purposeful
— that's how you get people hooked.'

IN THE GARDEN a man is picking flowers. It's a slightly odd sight, this burly young man gathering armfuls of larkspur and cosmos, slowly, with great concentration. There's something else odd, too, that takes a moment to register. The man has no legs — or none, at least, of flesh and bone. The deliberation of his movement is because he is learning to walk on new prosthetic limbs. Gathering the flowers, he has to spread his weight, to reach out, to balance. For the moment he's not thinking about it, absorbed in making up a pleasing bouquet to take home to his wife later that day.

'I call it therapy by stealth,' says Carol Sales, smiling.

Carol is in charge of the garden at Headley Court in Surrey, where her horticultural skills play a key part in the recovery of the injured servicemen and women undergoing treatment at the Defence and National Rehabilitation Centre. Their injuries are legion, sustained from training accidents and motorbike crashes, from parachute failures and botched landings, but most dramatically from service in Iraq and Afghanistan. Flown out from combat zones and patched up in Birmingham, this is where the most critically injured come to begin months, sometimes years, of therapy. The first triple amputee was admitted in 2008; since then there have been many more. Men and women who would certainly have died of their injuries just a decade ago now have a much greater chance of survival.

Carol's garden, all unmarshalled abundance, offers precious relief from the sterile hospital environment.

The task at Headley Court is to try to rebuild, as far as possible, those shattered bodies and splintered minds; to begin the painful process of remaking lives blown sky-high.

The cut flowers, all grown by patients from seed, are a recent project. 'I like them to have things to take home that are nothing to do with rehab,' says Carol. An exercise like this can achieve all kinds of physical goals – increasing standing tolerance and balance, improving concentration and hand-eye coordination, but that's just the beginning. 'We'll also start looking at the creatures that are landing on the flowers, and thinking about how the plants have evolved – we're not just sowing pretty seeds, but exploring the science behind it. The garden becomes a place where people can feel normal; a chill-out zone with interesting things to do and see and learn about, things they would never have thought of in a million years.'

Carol's patients are referred to her individually by occupational therapists in the various hospital departments – such as Lower Limbs, Upper Limbs, Neurology or Complex Trauma. Rehab isn't for sissies – these men and women are hard at work from eight in the morning to five in the afternoon daily, and Carol has to carve

Patients are encouraged to touch, taste, smell – to rediscover simple sensory pleasures.

out slots in these punishing schedules. There will be clear physical objectives – to stand for longer, to focus for longer, to work on dexterity or mobility or speech. Neurological patients have social skills to relearn – how to communicate without being rude or inappropriate. But it is rarely clear-cut: nearly everyone who comes to Carol is, to a greater or lesser extent, a complex case. Someone who seems to be making a good recovery will suddenly have a meltdown. Someone who has returned from the front line unscathed will fall down the stairs and damage his back. 'Being in chronic pain, they find they can't keep a lid on it any more. Until then they have managed to bury all the horror they have witnessed but, in intense pain, it's no longer possible. It's my job then to normalize those feelings, to make them acceptable. In fact, if they didn't feel as they do, having been through such traumatic experiences, I'd be quite concerned.'

It's hard to picture what it must feel like to have to reimagine yourself entirely – to have to renegotiate every relationship; to lose not only your health, your strength, your looks, your physical fitness (an essential part of their identity for many of the patients), but your career, your place in the world, your friends, your family – for that, Carol observes, is exactly how a soldier thinks of his regiment, or an airman thinks of his crew. The world outside can feel more hostile than any war zone. 'One chap told me he dreads going home at weekends. When he's here, he said, he feels normal, because everyone is damaged in some way. When he goes home, he feels like a freak.'

Carol understands this loss of identity on a deeper level than most of us. 'I had a serious head injury about twenty years ago, so I have experienced what it's like to be on the floor and feel like your life is never going to be the same again,' she says. 'My speech was affected. I couldn't remember how to cook, or in which order to get dressed – I had to be told by my sixteen-year-old son to put my socks on first.

'I don't for one minute try to tell the patients that I know where they're coming from, because it's pointless, but I can relate to what it's like not to be able to do stuff. So I'll just say, "Be thankful for small things and take one step at a time. You'll have good days, and you'll have several crap days, but we're all here and you're our main focus, and you *will* get better. You can come here any time you like. Here is a place where you don't have to be happy or jolly or brave. And if there's anything I can do to help, just shout."'

To get into the garden at Headley Court, you pass a battery of low red-brick buildings, fronted by a pergola of stiff-backed hybrid teas, before turning suddenly between immensely tall and fat yew hedges that block out all sight and sound. These curve around to deliver you abruptly to the top of a vast walled garden. A shallow slope, graded into broad stone-edged terraces, steps down to a large, cruciform formal pool, fronted by a grandiose fountain. In days gone by, the story goes, it served as an RAF swimming pool, and chair-bound pilots would be wheeled down and ruthlessly tipped in. The walls, of a glossy dark red brick, are elaborated with crenellations, alcoves and turrets, and pierced by lofty gabled gateways. More yew hedges describe a curving path around the perimeter, encircling an orchard of apples, pears and plums. There are greenhouses, and raised beds full of vegetables, and fat, contented hens bickering bossily over a handful of tomatoes. It's reassuringly random – cosmos sprouting among the cabbages, courgettes sprawling over hay bales, stacks of hazel twigs in teetering piles – not too tidy, a proper working garden. Half a dozen pots of thyme perch on a low wall by the path, inviting passers-by to fondle and sniff. Wobbly plaits of onions and strings of jewel-bright chillies are hanging to dry from every available spot. It feels, in short, about as different from a military hospital as

you can get. Patients have likened that progress through the yew tunnel to Alice falling down the rabbit hole – like falling into a dream world, or a parallel universe.

It is a comment that makes Carol smile. She is determined to offer a contrast to the sterile clinical environment where the patients spend their days, to create a place bubbling over with visual, tactile and olfactory stimulus. The greenhouse, the hub of her empire, is stuffed to the gunwales with tomatoes and chillies, basil and aubergines: the rich, earthy smell when she opens the door is the ultimate antithesis to TCP. Everyone is encouraged to touch, to taste, to scratch and sniff. The patients will go scrumping for apples, or pick soft fruit which

OPPOSITE *The orchard is a favourite place for patients to steal away for some quiet time.*
LEFT *Home-grown garlic hanging up to dry in the greenhouse.*

they'll then turn into jam. The key thing, to Carol's mind, is to start her charges connecting with the world around them, to rekindle delight in small, everyday pleasures in as many ways as she can.

'I firmly believe that the further away we get from nature, from the land, the more unhappy we are.' (It's hard to imagine an environment more denatured than a camp on permanent alert in barren Helmand.) Through programmes tailored individually for the three to six weeks a time that the patient will be at Headley Court, she seeks to pull her patients back, to put them back in touch with the seasons, to help them understand that things change, but life goes on. Accepting this, they can respond both on the level of metaphor and with physical engagement.

'Why sow seeds that you may not be here to see grow? Because if you look around, you'll see what your mates did — if you don't sow those seeds now, they won't be able to enjoy more tomatoes, or more cutting flowers. Giving something back is a way of affirming your dignity.'

This is very much the thinking behind horticultural therapy, certainly according to Anna Baker Cresswell. She is the founder of HighGround, one of the charities (along with ABF The Soldiers' Charity and some generous individuals) that fund Carol's position at Headley Court.

'A lot is about transferable skills,' says Anna. 'Physio is just physio, and when the session's over, that's it. But if you can learn something here that you can take back to your own garden, stuff to do with your children, to feed yourself better, or just to get outdoors and relax, that's of lifelong benefit.' Anna also sees a larger purpose: 'A lot of people have lost their faith in humankind as a result of what they've done and seen, and horticultural therapy can give them back their curiosity about life. If you sow something, you can't help wondering how it will turn out. Looking forward, with hope and optimism, is part and parcel of gardening. It's the fact that the cycle of the garden never ends, that is so important about it.'

'Very quickly', explains Carol, 'I establish a relationship with the patient and work out what they like doing, and build a programme around that, governed by what needs doing at each stage of the year. The pattern is that they are here for a few weeks, go home on leave, then come back. So one patient this year chitted a batch of potatoes; on his next admission he planted them; on the next he earthed them up, and on his last one in September he harvested them and took some home.' Similarly, a stroke patient, potting on a two-inch chilli seedling in March, determined that it would represent his recovery: he went home in September with a great, glossy plant groaning with fruit.

Bruce shows Carol his digging skills during a HighGround horticultural therapy session.

'It's nice to give people some continuity when so much of their lives is in chaos. When they have no idea what's happening or what is going to happen, at least they can come here, see how their spuds and French beans are getting on, and see some progression.'

Ninety per cent of Carol's patients have never gardened before. Some come wildly keen to learn to grow their own, so she teaches them the basics — how to plant, sow and harvest; pest management; crop rotation. There's something, she thinks, in all the destruction they have witnessed that provokes a visceral desire to nurture, to provide. Others are here under orders, and make it brutally clear that they have no interest at all. In that case Carol, unruffled, will just offer them a sit-down and a cup of tea, and perhaps invite them to taste a tomato. And when they've tasted a tomato or two, they may be curious as to how she grows them. 'And so it begins,' she murmurs, with a smile.

Sometimes there's no growing at all, but foraging for chestnuts or puffballs or figs, or

Lee has been so smitten by the gardening bug that he has bought a smallholding in France.

simply going for a walk around the garden and seeing what they find. Looking at a leaf, she can gently instruct on the processes of transpiration and photosynthesis; finding a colony of broomrapes in the grass sparks a lesson on parasitic plants and how and why they don't photosynthesize. Another day, she might suggest making something from hazel wands — a plant support for the garden, or a swag for the mantelpiece. Last Christmas, she recalls, the word about the hazel got around, and before she knew it she had nine strapping lads in the greenhouse, all busy with raffia and florist's wire, delicately tucking in foliage and berries to make wreaths for their front doors.

The range of her skills is humbling — she must be gardener, craftsman, educator, botanist, hen-keeper, cook, counsellor and, in many cases, surrogate mum.

'She's a one-off,' says Anna, simply. And her patients are inclined to agree.

For forty-four-year-old Lee, Carol's input has been life-changing. Despite two years on crutches, the threat of losing his leg (he has had sixteen operations to his legs and hips) and ongoing post-traumatic stress disorder, he is determined to move to France and start a smallholding, keeping animals and growing his own food.

'If you'd have said that two years ago I'd have laughed,' he says. 'Me, turn into a tree-hugger? I used to mock my dad in his greenhouse. But after that first hour with Carol I went back to my room all fired up. I only wish I'd done it twenty years ago. The whole sector appeals to me – the science, the technical know-how behind it. I'm on YouTube every night learning how to do things – propagating, composting; I'm even distilling my own spirits. *Home Farmer* magazine has become my version of porn.

'It's good to find out what you can still do physically, how to make the best of the situation,' he continues. 'And mentally, I find the gardening calms me down, it helps me to focus and gives me some release from the drudgery of constant pain.'

Gardening skills are, in a way, the least important things he has learned with Carol. Safe in the greenhouse, Lee discovered that life wasn't over, but starting afresh.

'Though many of my patients struggle to see it at first, I tell them that this is an exciting time for them,' says Carol. 'They have their whole future ahead of them. They've had a career and now they have a second chance to do something completely different and find something they really like. After years in the military, it's an opportunity to discover what they like to eat, to do, to wear – who they really are. They're going to end up in a better place, doing something they love, having time with their kids and watching them grow up.'

———◆———

Carol came to Headley Court after escaping from prison. Actually, it wasn't an escape, she adds quickly; she loved working with prisoners, and she can see many similarities between the two groups: a concentration of young men who have been institutionalized in one way or another, a very macho culture, a lot of anger and frustration. At Coldingley, a resettlement prison in Surrey, she set up a horticultural training scheme, preparing participants to sit City & Guilds qualifications. She even had them learning botanical Latin. When others mocked, saying the prisoners could barely speak English, she would firmly point out that she herself had not had any horticultural qualifications until her mid-forties, and only acquired a degree at the age of fifty. It's never too late to learn.

Carol grew up in a flat in London. There was no garden, but she was always fascinated by plants, even as a tiny child. But her family didn't consider gardening a proper job: on leaving school, she spent seven dreary years in a bank. She was married

at twenty ('Far too young, it ought to be illegal') and pregnant with her first child at twenty-three. Having moved out to the country, she started gardening and by the time her second son came along, she was tending a large ornamental garden and growing all the family's food.

Her irritation at a notice in the village shop:

WANTED, RELIABLE MAN FOR GARDENING. TWO HOURS A WEEK.

jump-started her into action. 'I rang them up and said, "I'm not a man but I *am* reliable." That was the start of it. I was young and fit, and I learned my gardening by doing.'

'When they go home, especially the wheelchair-bound and the amputees, they often just sit indoors and won't go out. So I show them how easy it is to look after chickens. The eggs are nutritious, it's great for the kids, and it forces them to go outside, to care for the birds.'

When her children were small, she would take them to pick strawberries in a nearby walled garden. She was offered two weeks' holiday cover; ten years later she was still there. She became head gardener, growing heritage apples, pears and peaches, all manner of soft fruit and over ninety varieties of flowers for drying – delphiniums, peonies and more than a thousand roses.

When her employer retired and the garden was sold, she moved on to work for a landscaper. 'I was encouraging one of the younger lads to get qualified, when I had a light bulb moment – I realized I didn't have any qualifications myself.' She enrolled at Chichester College in West Sussex to study horticulture and garden design. So outstanding were her results that the college invited her to join the teaching staff, offering her classes one day a week. 'That was on December sixteenth, I remember. My boss had just closed the business and made everybody redundant. I was on my own by then, recently divorced, with two boys to support through college. I decided we'd have a decent Christmas and I wouldn't panic about it till the fifth of January, and on the sixth I launched my own garden design and landscaping business.' She went on to take a teaching degree, taught at various colleges and became a workplace assessor, before being invited to Coldingley.

Moving on to Headley Court wasn't an easy decision. 'I had to think about it carefully because I took quite a big cut in salary, and I really loved working with the prisoners. But I thought it would be a new challenge, as I'm the only

First stop for every 'Mr Angry' is a visit to the garden's flock of hens. It makes Carol smile to see how a small fluffy chicken will melt the heart of the most battle-hardened squaddie.

horticulturist in the country working with serving military — and I could make it my own. Hopefully, that's what I've achieved.'

The hardest part in many ways is accepting the limits of what she can do. A successful day, to her mind, is when someone arrives feeling lousy and leaves happy and smiling, or when someone achieves something they didn't think they could. She's still laughing about a recent incident when a soldier reported as unable to walk got out of his wheelchair and pushed it up the hill. 'It was like Lazarus,' she giggles, wiping the tears from her eyes. It's a success when she can send someone home with some newly laid eggs and a handful of courgettes, so the family can make an omelette together; or perhaps some tomato plants that the children will care for next time their mum or dad is admitted. 'It's so important to find ways of re-engaging with partners and children, because if people have been away a lot on tour or in hospital, they can feel they've lost that connection with the family.'

Most of her patients can never return to duty. (That's where HighGround comes in, offering employment opportunities and training in the land-based sector.) It can be hard for them to accept what their options and limitations will be. Carol has to watch and wait while the realization dawns that a job as a bodyguard or an oil rig worker, or whatever they have set their heart on, simply isn't physically possible.

'It's especially hard for the older patients to transition from the forces,' she says.

'They might have joined up at sixteen or eighteen, so they don't develop socially in the same way as everyone else; they miss out on that late teenage/early twenties bit — going out and mixing with other people. That often makes people scared of civilians — they feel that civvies don't like them. So some of the work I do is about reintegrating people into society.' She has found trips to Hampton Court Palace Flower Show or the garden at RHS Wisley effective in that they expose patients to other people, but on their own terms. Where once the fear of crowds, of not knowing where the exits are, and the abiding terror of being taken hostage would have made it impossible for the patients to relax, the atmosphere of a garden — and even simply the mental image of it — reduces the stress of hyper-vigilance (a classic symptom of PTSD) and helps them manage difficult moments.

Depression, inevitably, is common; even despair. 'Then I try to focus on the positives in their lives; I try to get them to value what they do have. Plants are a powerful vector,' she says. 'I've seen incredible progress in as little as a week.'

Sometimes, she admits, it's hard not to be overwhelmed by the pity of it, the rage, the frustration, the dogged courage, the terrible sense of loss. There are days, she confesses, she just goes home and cries. 'But whatever I feel, I have to put it on the back burner.'

For bodies and minds traumatized by extreme violence, relearning delicate hand skills is an important step. Careful tasks like threading chillies and pricking out require both dexterity and concentration.

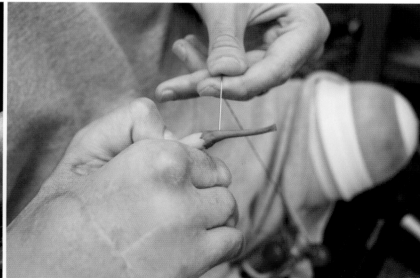

And that, of course, is how therapists have to operate. Only, gardeners are hard-wired to nurture. Above Carol's little desk in a corner of the greenhouse is a brightly coloured thank-you card, shakily inscribed with her name. Inside is a photograph of a pale-cheeked boy holding a small fluffy hen up to his face. 'We call that hen The Bearded Lady,' says Carol. 'That made him laugh. He was stroking her feathers and put his face on her and it was just one of those moments . . . He's confined to a wheelchair, with limited speech and very limited mobility – to write that card and to bring it to me here was an enormous thing for him.' She busies herself abruptly with a fuchsia. 'I didn't know what to say – I had to go and have a quiet moment. He's a beautiful boy,' she says softly, 'and it's terrible what's happened to him.'

Headley Court is due to be disbanded, to move to state-of-the-art new premises in the Midlands. Carol will not be transferring with it. 'It makes me sad,' she says. 'I can think of nothing better than staying on here, bringing more people to horticulture and demystifying it. If I could have one wish, I'd love the people I have worked with to get in touch and let me know how they're doing. We've shared part of a difficult journey. I'd like to know that they're OK.'

Juicy home-grown tomatoes are Carol's secret weapon for tempting recalcitrant patients to take an interest in growing.

PLANTING FOR POSTERITY

ANDREW WOODALL
Broughton Grange, Oxfordshire

'My philosophy is that every year the gardens should look better than they did the year before. It's not always possible — sometimes the weather and the seasons are against you — but that has to be your goal.'

ASK ANDREW WOODALL what qualities he looks for in a gardener, and he doesn't hesitate for a second. 'Passion!' he declares. For gardening, to his mind, is not so much a career as a lifestyle choice, and it's only if you live and breathe it that you'll put up with the long hours, the low pay, the lack of status, the sheer uncoolness of it; for gardening, in Britain at least, is overwhelmingly the domain of doddery, retired gentlefolk. (It's not at all like that, he points out indignantly, in Scandinavia, whence hail many strapping, radiant twenty-somethings who come to visit the garden.) It also helps to be funny. On cold, wet days, of which there are all too many, it's humour that gets you through. He likes easy-going people who will bond to make a team, and in return will feel needed and wanted: he can't think of anything more miserable than being a sole gardener. And it helps to know a strimmer from a leaf blower: he's still scratching his head over a work placement student who proved unable to identify either. There's a lot of machinery at Broughton Grange: even the bulbs are planted with a petrol augur. But then, you could hardly plant five thousand tulip bulbs in a single day with a trowel.

Andrew is a great believer in the university of life, so few of his team have formal horticultural credentials. He, however, had a proper old-fashioned training of a kind that is now rare, apprenticed at sixteen to Paul Witney, head gardener at

St Anne's College, Oxford (then an all-female college). Witney had spent years at Lawrence Johnston's acclaimed garden at Hidcote in Gloucestershire, and instilled the highest standards in his young apprentice — the only one, it turns out, to have stuck with gardening. Perhaps the other lads found being surrounded by two hundred noisy young women too distracting. Andrew claims not to have noticed. Thereafter, he did a stint in commercial horticulture, before returning to college in his twenties. But his progress, he'd be the first to say, has less to do with passing exams than sheer serendipity. He would say he's been a very lucky man.

He did not have the best start in life, his father having departed and his mother fallen ill, meaning that at just two years old he and his twin brother were lodged with foster parents. Soon after, his foster mother lost her own husband and son, and subsequently devoted the rest of her life (she was already fifty-three when they arrived) to the two little boys in her care. She taught them to love nature, especially birds. Like Paul Pulford, the young Andrew was a devoted ornithologist and egg collector. She grew flowers and vegetables in her big Thames-side garden, and by eleven Andrew was already a willing and proficient helper. Their neighbour, however, had a much more impressive veg plot, so at critical times a cricket ball would sail 'accidentally' over the fence, so that the young gardener could sneak a closer look (and taste). 'She was a marvellous woman, and while she didn't push me, she could tell I had a passion for plants from very early on, and encouraged me to consider horticulture as a career.'

Luck smiled again over a bowl of porridge on a Greek beach. The gorgeous young Dane so inauspiciously wooed eventually became Andrew's wife. 'Charlotte is my rock,' he avows, in an unabashed, smiling, actually rather Danish kind of a way. Whatever success he has enjoyed in his career he attributes entirely to her loyalty, pragmatism and good sense.

But to some extent you make your own luck — at least if that consists in seeing an opportunity, and not being afraid to grab it. One evening, browsing idly on the English Country Gardeners website (who doesn't look at the job ads now and again?), he saw a position advertised in Tuscany — designer Arabella Lennox-Boyd wanted an English head gardener to work alongside her on a new garden she was making there. 'It was just pure chance that I saw it. But I thought, "Right, let's load the guns and go for it."'

It wasn't quite as simple as that. It took fourteen months, seven interviews, a full medical and even an analysis of his handwriting before they offered him the job. But in the autumn of 2003, he and Charlotte loaded up a truck with lock, stock, barrel, small son and dog, and set off for Il Palagio.

Andrew is someone who is comfortable with risk.

Andrew was no stranger to risk taking. After St Anne's, he had spent three years in a chrysanthemum nursery, then moved to Holland for two years. Returning to England, he drew on his Dutch experience to set up a series of enterprises — working on stilts tending commercial glass houses, growing strawberries, even farming snails. He then abandoned the lot to go to Hadlow College and get his qualifications. His first head gardener appointment was in 1992, at Pennington House near Lymington — a run-down garden that required total renovation. He wasn't daunted: 'I rather like the challenge of an empty canvas. You can start small and make it up as you go along. It doesn't have to be overwhelming.

'I thought I would be there all my life. I was happy there, it was challenging enough, and the garden was big enough. And then in 1998 my son was born, and that changed everything. I suddenly realized, "Hang on a minute, this is a whole new chapter …"'

'Anyone's design is only as good as the people who look after it.
When I leave and the next head gardener comes along,
I wonder how they will perceive it and what changes they
will make? It's not something to worry about.
That's what gardening is about.'

From Lymington he moved to Fort Belvedere in Surrey, the
former royal residence where Edward VIII had lived with Wallis
Simpson, and where he signed his abdication papers. Andrew's
employers were the Westons, high society owners of London
department stores Selfridges and Fortnum & Mason, but he had
little direct contact with them. The chain of command was long
and circuitous, the property was occupied only for the summer
season, just eight to ten weeks a year, and the grand, rather
formal garden was rarely seen by anyone but the family. The
exception was a huge birthday party in 2003. 'It was dubbed the
"Party of the Decade"', recalls Andrew. 'There were 360 guests,
all kinds of celebrities, even the Queen. And I have to say the
garden was looking a picture. When I heard that the Queen had
commented that the gardens were looking amazing, I felt I'd
reached my peak there, and that I should leave on a high. So you
might say it was the Queen who sent me on my way to Italy ...'

Il Palagio was a sixteenth-century villa set among the
vineyards and olive groves of the hills south of Florence. The
owners were the musician Sting and his designer wife Trudie
Styler, who were deeply involved in bringing the dilapidated
estate back into fruitful production, but who circumspectly
left the garden development in the ferociously competent
hands of Lennox-Boyd. It was hard work for Andrew: building
new terraces, persuading transplanted olive trees to survive in
their new homes, establishing lawns and a rose garden against
the odds. Despite the rich history of Italian gardens, there is
nothing comparable to the British tradition of plantsmanship
and horticultural craftsmanship, so training local staff took
supreme patience and determination. Then Charlotte, unable

Andrew's favourite relaxation is to set off on his bike, especially on a long summer's evening.

to find work and fed up with being marooned in a tiny hilltop village, eventually returned to England for term times. So it was long, hot, gruelling and often lonely work for the further two and half years it took to finish the job. For all that, he doesn't regret a day of it.

'It was an education working with Arabella; I learned so much from observing her — her amazing eye for detail, and how she could anticipate quite little things that would make a big difference in a garden. It was a wonderful experience, but I knew that at some point I'd have to come back. When Broughton Grange popped up it ticked all the boxes — I could apply everything I'd learned and bring it here, and see this garden through to its next phase.'

Broughton Grange hit the horticultural big time following the creation of a truly innovative walled garden, designed by Tom Stuart-Smith in 2001. It is unusual in a number of respects — first, that it is entirely divorced from the house; second, its irregular division into three terraces of markedly different character; and, third, that it is walled on only two sides and visually linked, with extraordinary subtlety and skill, with the undulating north Oxfordshire landscape that unrolls all around it.

The planting is spectacular, largely shrubby and Mediterranean on the top level, rubbing shoulders comfortably with fruit and veg and well-stocked glasshouses. The middle level is taller and wispier, juxtaposed with a broad, rectangular pool that hooks down to earth a wide slice of sky. The third terrace is quite different – a wobbly box parterre representing the cellular structure of the beech, ash and oak trees that grow on the estate (Stuart-Smith enjoys a good intellectual conceit), bedded out with tulips in spring and in summer with gorgeous puddles of colour which Andrew likes to vary year by year.

It deserves its press – it truly is a garden that works all year round: richly hued billowing abundance in summer; delicate and sepia-toned in winter. Andrew likes it best in late September, when the light becomes pearly and the shadows long, and the honeyed tones of ripening grasses connect most strongly to the golden fields below. But there is a lot, lot more to Broughton Grange than this: namely twenty further acres in an extraordinary hotchpotch of styles – a knot garden and formal parterre that curtsey to the gabled Victorian house, traditional long borders in the

The curved shapes of the parterre, OPPOSITE, *based on the cellular structure of three native trees, are a boon to the gardener – much more forgiving of the odd nick than the more usual geometric shapes, as* BELOW.

Cotswold manor house idiom (if marginally less genteel), ornamental woodland, fashionable wild flower and water meadows and a semi-wild spring walk, alongside quirkier features such as a peat-block garden, a bamboo garden and a deliciously Gormenghastish stumpery, all blackened roots and brooding ferns. There is one of the prettiest pool gardens you'll ever see, that could almost persuade you you're in the Med. There is a laburnum tunnel that, frankly, makes Rosemary Verey's efforts at Barnsley House look puny. And, in addition to all this, a hugely ambitious new arboretum has been taking shape since 2008 (once it was acknowledged that the original thirty-acre site to the south of the garden could not accommodate a single tree more.) It currently stands at fifty acres and around fifteen hundred trees, rolling out to the skyline as far as the eye can see, and is, Andrew believes, the most extensive ornamental planting to take place in Britain for the last hundred years.

It is the most phenomenal amount of work. Every specimen is grown on for two full years before being planted out, yet those fifty or hundred trees that look so substantial in Andrew's tree nursery somehow melt away to nothing when he places them out in the landscape. Each new planting is carefully weeded, thickly mulched with herbicide granules and bark, netted against rabbits and deer, then irrigated for the first two years, which means labour-intensive individual watering

from a bowser with a hose. Thereafter the young trees are generally left unwatered, to encourage deeper-searching roots. Each specimen is logged on a database and mapped with GPS to enable long-term monitoring, but day to day they rely on the use of different coloured netting for each year's plantings to ensure that none of the saplings is missed. It takes one week to cut the flower-rich grass with a tractor; then strimming around each tree takes two men five days. And all this must be fitted between regular garden work, and before the great autumn clear-up that starts in October. It is exciting, elating, to be place-making on this scale, like a latter-day Capability Brown, but it's tough going without a Capability Brown sized workforce.

It's a classic conundrum, reconciling the needs and wants of a garden's owner with the art of the possible ... Of all the tools in the head gardener's bothy, the most skilfully deployed is diplomacy. Andrew has been in private service virtually all his life. Generally, that means freedom from the pettifogging bureaucracy that often beleaguers the public and charitable sector. The pay is usually better, and the garden budget more generous. But it comes with its own set of problems.

OPPOSITE *The planting of the walled garden, open on two sides, seeks to form a connection with the surrounding landscape.*
BELOW *The arboretum is one of the largest planted in Britain since the eighteenth century, when tree planting was regarded as a patriotic duty.*

In a garden administered by a local authority or the heritage sector, the chain of command may be long and slow, but at least it is clear. However, where a private garden is one of several, and the owners are only fleetingly resident, the head gardener may have to report to a property manager, accountant or some other personage who may or may not control the purse strings, and who may or may not have an interest in the garden. So it can be just as difficult to get quick decisions, and virtually impossible to implement change.

'Trees are the best monuments that a man can erect to his own memory. They speak his praises without flattery, and they are blessings to children yet unborn.'

LORD ORRERY, 1749

Again, in a public garden, the primary function of the garden is plain: to delight the visitors. But in each place that Andrew has worked, he has had to ask himself the question: 'What is this garden for?' Is it essentially an ornamental backdrop for parties? A meeting place? A stage set? And, most importantly, does anyone really care about this garden, or is it just an exercise in conspicuous consumption, the vegetable equivalent of the BMW and the Rolex watch?

That may not be a bad thing: indifferent owners may willingly give their gardener complete autonomy – lack of appreciation might be a price well worth paying for a free hand. On the other hand, non-gardeners rarely understand the amount of work involved in maintaining a garden. (At Broughton Grange, Andrew presents a written report every Friday detailing what has been done and the work planned for the next week.) Conversely, a keen owner may be tempted to micromanage. And what happens when a designer is brought in? Who is the ultimate decision-maker now? The owner who commissioned the design, the designer who dreamed it up, or the head gardener who must implement and maintain it? The walled garden at Broughton Grange is routinely described as 'a Tom Stuart-Smith garden', but after ten years of editing, isn't it just as much an 'Andrew Woodall' garden? And if owner Stephen Hester wants to make a change, does he feel he must seek either man's agreement?

It seems unlikely: high achievers in any field rarely get there without a hefty dollop of self-confidence. And there are definitely traces of megalomania in this garden: WHY make a garden out of blocks of peat just to grow azaleas that don't want to grow here? WHY site a stumpery for shade-loving plants facing due south? The sun was a problem to start with, concedes Andrew, but some fast-growing catalpas soon did the trick, and the stumpery is now his favourite spot. (It seems this obduracy in the face of nature may, in fact, be Andrew's.) 'Besides,' he says cheerfully, 'what I like about gardening is that you learn by your mistakes and you move forward. There's not much that's irreversible.'

A serpentine path in the arboretum seems to lead to the skyline.

That, of course, is taking the long view. It comes naturally to gardeners. This includes Hester, who is busy planting trees that he will never see mature – standard practice among the landed classes in previous centuries, but a notion that seems increasingly quaint in our 'have-it-all, have-it-now' society. Formerly the controversial CEO of the Royal Bank of Scotland, Hester no doubt understands something of the fleetingness of reputation and riches (not that he appears to be on his uppers), and are not trees, as Lord Orrery wrote in 1749, 'the best monuments that a man can erect to his own memory'?

It is this sense of creating something lasting, something significant, that sets Broughton Grange apart from the other gardens Andrew has worked in. He observes with satisfaction that the garden has taken on its own momentum, that although it remains a source of private pleasure, its fame has spread all over the world. Few weeks pass without a tour, and with his laid-back manner and ready chat, Andrew makes an engaging guide.

'Give it another ten to fifteen years and Broughton Grange will be memorable,' he promises. 'It is already being compared with Hidcote, and there's still plenty of room to develop it further: the infrastructure is there to make it one of the most stunning gardens of the century. Even after fifteen years, it's still considered a very modern garden, so it will be interesting to see how it stands in years to come. The important thing is not to overdo it. The garden will develop under its own steam, and doesn't need to be more diverse than it is. It's more about adjusting small areas to make them better and better. Gardens shouldn't change too quickly, but every year should look better than the last.'

They have recently started opening on Wednesdays from May to September, and so far Andrew is delighted. 'Making a garden on this scale that no one ever sees is like an artist painting a picture, then hiding it away in the attic. Sharing it encourages us to do our job well.' It doesn't mean a lot more work (they get someone in to do the tea and cake), and he's not under the same pressure as gardens that open daily: if he wants to get on with a noisy job, or leave clippings scattered on the path, there are plenty of days when he can. But it won't be long before he'll have to start thinking about lavatories and car parks, which both staff and family must learn to look on not as an intrusion, but a necessary first step towards making the garden financially sustainable. It's a touch disappointing – that even the cherished project of a garden-obsessed banker with a big estate and even bigger ideas might be subject to budgetary restraints …

With 80 acres to care for, it's essential for Andrew to get jobs done quickly wherever he can. (Besides, he does rather like Boys' Toys.)

'It's always the case,' says Andrew. Having worked with million-pound budgets, and for both new money and old, he should know. The best you can hope for is a wealthy individual who is genuinely interested in the garden, with enough imagination to want it to develop, enough cash to enact what is needed, and the humility and common sense to give his head gardener free rein. 'I treat this as my own garden,' says Andrew, 'although I know it's not. But to have a job where you love what you do and know you're going to have it for the rest of your life — that's contentment.'

'A garden on this scale that no one ever sees is like an artist painting a picture, then hiding it away in the attic.'

If that sounds like a glib statement, it isn't. There is not a glimmer of complacency about the man — he is clearly a striver, enterprising, ambitious.

With Andrew you feel that contentment has been hard won. He met his birth mother again when he was eight, and saw her regularly until she died, but she remained a fragile, peripheral figure in his life. He regrets that he never got to know his father — he knew little of his life till after he died. So it is entirely understandable that family should be his anchor and, as he puts it, 'the reserve fuel tank that made me want to achieve, to do well'. It is good to have reached the knowledge that he is doing the right thing, and in the right place. But he still seems to need to prove himself, to show himself worthy.

In 2013, to celebrate his fiftieth birthday, he resolved to cycle from Land's End to John O'Groats, accompanied by his twin. On just the second day his brother had to pull out, and he was left on his own, up on Bodmin Moor in the lashing rain, with sixty miles still to cycle before nightfall. The disappointment was crushing, and no one would have blamed him if he'd given up, at least for the day, and put his bike on the train. But he kept on going. And he went on going all the way to the end, cycling 998 miles over fifteen days. 'I'd planned it all for such a long time,' he says, 'and I didn't want to fail.' His family joined him for the last leg, and it was with his son that he cycled the last few miles to the sea. 'I cried my eyes out when I got there,' he confesses. He remembers it as one of the best days of his life.

'It was one of those life experiences that make you,' he says. And as he looks back over his life, with all its challenges, self-inflicted and otherwise, he can honestly say, there isn't much he'd change. 'There's nothing I regret. There's nothing I've done that I wish I hadn't done — it's all the things I have done that make me who I am.'

To be who you are, and not to wish to be different; that's contentment. And not a bad legacy — at least as good as a tree — to leave to your child.

STUMPERY

PEAT BLOCK GARDEN

KNOT GARDEN

LONG BORDERS

PARTERRE

SUNDRIES
FOLDER 2.

Burrows Nursery
FM plc + Sons.
Sign Company
ERIC Hunter
Hozzard Horticulture
LBS
Rigby Taylor
Pear

First Aid / Safety
supplys
BANBURY FARM
got ed
Greentech
RHS
BANBURY turf.

STAPLES
FOLDER 1.

HORTICULTURAL
SUNDRIES –
Website / phone
printing
cost + Carry
Loo Hire
P&P
Global parasols
TECHTONICS
GRAMOGRAPH
Teracraft
Amaro

STAPLES

PLANTS

TREES

BULBS

SEED

PLANTS.

8000998

MADE IN ENGLAND

STAPLES

FOLDER 1.

HOUSEHOLD

Congestion
Charges.
CROXSONS Bottles
Vigo
Chris Alvarez
Janet Alvarez
DESIGNS.
BT
Mercross
Lodge Security
N power
White food recipts

8000998

MADE IN ENGLAND

THE SHOW
MUST GO ON

MICHAEL WALKER
Trentham Gardens, Staffordshire

'Looking after a garden and estate takes lots of different things —
first financial support, then vision and, definitely, enthusiasm.'

THERE IS A FAMOUS letter from the greatest of nineteenth-century
gardeners, Joseph Paxton, in which he tells of his arrival at Chatsworth House
in Derbyshire in May 1826, aged just twenty-three, to take up his new post as head
gardener. Arriving at half past four in the morning, he finds, unsurprisingly, that
there's no one about, so he climbs in over the greenhouse gate for a recce:

> [I] explored the pleasure grounds and looked round the outside of the house.
> I then went down to the kitchen gardens, scaled the outside wall and saw the
> whole of the place, set the men to work there at six o'clock; then returned
> to Chatsworth and got Thomas Weldon to play me the water works and
> afterwards went to breakfast with poor dear Mrs Gregory and her niece. The
> latter fell in love with me and I with her and thus completed my first morning's
> work at Chatsworth before nine o'clock.

There is more than one echo of Paxton in the life of Michael Walker, now officially
titled Head of Garden and Estate at the Trentham Estate in Staffordshire. He has
that self-same dash and energy, the same disinclination to let petty barriers impede
him. And he is equally decisive in matters of the heart: arriving on secondment to
Powis Castle in 1983, he had identified his future wife by lunchtime. The night

before taking up his first head gardener post, at Beningbrough Hall in Yorkshire, he too made a clandestine visit. 'I was determined to start with a bang,' he recalls, shaking with incredulous laughter at his twenty-two-year-old self. 'What I wanted was to march straight in with a big list of things that needed doing.' He was crestfallen to find the garden in such fine shape, he couldn't think of a single intervention. 'So I had to start my new job by asking the staff what *they* thought was needed. Now of course I know that's exactly the right thing to do.'

He looks back now with wonderment at being head gardener at so tender an age. 'I wasn't a very good one,' he says frankly. 'But I learned as I went along.' Indeed, the National Trust's youngest head gardener soon developed a reputation as an *enfant terrible,* falling out with his regional manager within a month when threatened with a budget cut, or having conniptions when dodgems appeared in his walled garden. 'Dodgems!' he growls. His outrage has not mellowed one jot in three decades. He was, he confesses, an 'angry young man', anxious for more autonomy, more money, more status. 'My manager soon started pointing out all these wonderful jobs in different regions ... But now I look back with such fond memories to Beningbrough as the best place I ever worked. People were so kind to me, this young Ulster lad a long way from home: they took me under their wing. That's where I learned what I was good at — getting gardens to move forward.

Restoring Charles Barry's epic terraces was a colossal challenge — every element needed rebuilding.

'In those days there weren't garden historians dripping from the trees, and the head gardener's job was simply to make the garden a better setting for the house, and more attractive to visitors,' says Michael. 'But by understanding its past, you could present it in a much more interesting way. Then, by considering where your garden stood in the roster of attractions in an area, you could try to find something more exciting or more significant to offer your visitors. It's important for a head gardener to be commercially aware.'

It's this breadth of vision that has carried Michael to the very top of his profession, responsible for a sequence of prestigious garden restorations; in demand as adviser, mentor and champion; hugely respected for his technical expertise, his boundless energy and what are known in management-speak as 'leadership qualities'.

In the Edwardian heyday of the great country estate, employers would advertise for 'working' or 'non-working' head gardeners, the second category no longer required to wield a spade, but to manage substantial land holdings and a large and complex workforce. It is this category that Michael Walker embodies today. 'I loved the hands-on role when I started but I don't miss it – I certainly don't have any regrets that my role has become more managerial. I'm very project-orientated, and I love the diversity of the role. I no longer get my hands dirty, but that's a very conscious decision I made quite a long time ago.'

His broad face seems constantly wreathed in smiles. His strong Ulster accent is rhythmic and avuncular. Showing off his garden, there's nothing pat or rehearsed about his delivery – his enthusiasm is unfeigned. He actually seems to like his visitors, exchanging merry greetings, giggling out loud at a fat and cartoonish dog, and rushing to assist a small bedraggled sprite in fairy wings who has tripped over her own feet and is sprawling in the gravel. As he lifts her to her feet, she immediately stops crying. Her mum smiles gratefully. People like Michael Walker.

This, of course, is how he gets things done. He doesn't set out to charm in any calculated way: he just wins people over by his simple warmth and niceness. Then before they know it, they are whisked along by the sheer force of his energy and enthusiasm. He is not, he admits, the most patient of men. 'I always want the next thing to happen tomorrow. I don't embark on a five-year plan expecting to deliver the last bit in year five – I want it all in year one. I love momentum. I've seen so many projects that have run out of puff after the initial stage, through the inertia built into large and complicated organizations. So if I do have any patience, perhaps that's where it lies, in negotiating and carrying people with me.'

Sometimes, he knows, the people he works with seem to be pulling him back with ropes, and then he must back down and be guided by their expertise. 'But sometimes you just believe in something and say, I'm going to do this regardless, and then you

A chart shows the highlights of Michael's new conservation plan to restore Trentham's lost Capability Brown landscape.

must find ways to achieve it. I'm like a terrier: I never give up. I'll go back and back, trying different ways to get something through.

'I think that people find me quite demanding to work for and probably quite frustrating too, but the proof of the pudding is we deliver our targets and we achieve great things together — just as we're doing here at Trentham.'

———◆———

Trentham has always been a showpiece, at the cutting edge of horticultural fashion. By the early eighteenth century, the former Augustinian priory sat grandly within an extensive formal landscape. This was remodelled from 1759 by Capability Brown, who enlarged the lake and surrounded it with rolling parkland. Seventy years later, society architect Charles Barry (who went on to design both the Palace of Westminster and Highclere Castle, aka Downton Abbey) was called in to transform the house into an Italian palazzo, with a grandiose garden to match. Harriet, Duchess of Sutherland, had a passion for gardening (not just at Trentham but at her other houses at Cliveden, Berkshire, and in Scotland) which tested even the Sutherlands' epic resources. Given carte blanche by Harriet, Barry created an immense terraced garden between the house and the lake, linked by steps and broad gravel walks, elaborately decorated with urns and balustrades, fountains and pavilions and ornate stone-edged parterres. It became, for decades, the most fashionable garden in England, Barry's opulent architecture providing an ample canvas for the horticultural experiments of Trentham's pioneering head gardener, George Fleming.

Fleming was a man of great resourcefulness. When he needed a heating system for a lofty new conservatory, or a machine to speed up weeding, or a device for transplanting mature trees, he got on and invented them himself. And when pollution from the River Trent threatened to overwhelm Brown's great lake, he thought nothing of diverting the river and finding alternative ways to maintain the water level. But what he is chiefly remembered for today is his development of an exciting new planting technique — bedding out.

There is a wonderful picture book of 1857, E. Adveno Brooke's *The Gardens of England*, that shows Trentham at its zenith — resplendent exemplar of the garden style that was to define the Victorian era. Scarlet pelargoniums cascade in profusion from

The statue of Perseus is a copy of Benvenuto Cellini's famous Renaissance bronze in Florence.

mighty urns; crinolined ladies stroll along broad paths flanked by long, parallel ribbons of colour – blue, red, green and yellow. A view along a highly decorated border is framed by a circular trellis-work window, wreathed with fat pink roses. It is a confident, theatrical style, perfectly in keeping with the zeitgeist, and full of promise for an adventurous gardener. For here was a whole new category of plant material, summoned from distant corners of the empire, suddenly made accessible through a series of technological and economic developments – railway transport, affordable glasshouses, cheap coal and cheap labour. Here were new forms, new textures and, above all, brilliant new colours. Thinking about how best to employ that colour became the crucial horticultural concern of the time.

Along with Donald Beaton, head gardener at Shrubland Hall in Suffolk and a keen contributor to the new horticultural magazines, Fleming became the leading exponent of colour theory, demonstrating at Trentham the principles Beaton set out in his writings. Today we are inclined to dismiss bedding as crude and strident, but these two enquiring head gardeners were exploring 'harmony of colour' as well as 'the true definition of contrast'; thinking about how to use different heights and

The flat patterning of the immense parterre is given lift and rhythm by columns of yew.

proportions, and how best to 'blend the trailing with the erect species' – techniques we now take for granted every time we plant a summer tub. Some of these effects were bold – the Ribbon Borders, developed here, with continuous lines of colour extending their whole length, or the Rainbow Walk made in the 1850s, planted, as its name suggests, in rainbow colours. But Fleming also created the charming 'rivulet', a serpentine bed of forget-me-nots resembling a meandering stream; introduced foliage plants for more subtle and enduring effects; and experimented with 'shading', planting so that one colour would merge subtly into another, paving the way for another great colourist, Gertrude Jekyll.

'I have a little knowledge. I've never professed to be an expert in anything I've done.'

This was work on a massive scale, not least since there were constant new refinements in the borders: 'Every year they are diversified,' wrote one visitor, 'every year more expressive; and the thousands of plants required in its decoration brings the arrangement to a gigantic scale.' Over one hundred thousand new plants a year were needed for the Italian Garden alone. By 1847, Fleming had a staff of forty-three gardeners, five labourers and seven plantation workers under him. He was also managing an immense kitchen garden and conducting mass plantings of rhododendrons in the park. This labour-intensive style was continued by his successor Archibald Stevenson in 1861, followed by equally lauded head gardener Zadock Stevens, and lasted till 1902, when seventy gardeners were dismissed.

By this time, Trentham had been abandoned by the family. The rapid expansion of the Potteries had led to appalling pollution, and while the changing displays of bedding held up well to these conditions, aristocratic noses could no longer endure it. The house was demolished in 1911, and the last head gardener, Peter Christie Blair, saw out his days in the fine gabled house built by Barry for Fleming in the kitchen garden, surrounded by the ruins of Trentham's once fabled glasshouses.

The incumbent Sutherlands had offered Trentham to the local authority as a public park, but under conditions that made it impossible to accept. Now they set about developing the redundant garden as a leisure facility for local people. There was golf and tennis and boating on the lake. By the 1930s there was also a lido, a miniature railway, and a magnificent Art Deco ballroom, demolished only in 2004 to make way for today's garden centre.

The gardens did not fare well. The Capability Brown park was overlaid with commercial forestry, except for the area that was a caravan park. The annual Lombard RAC rally roared through the woodlands, around the lake and cut straight through the Italian Garden. Bits of the estate subsided, thanks to mining activity: in 1975 the lido had to be closed when the lake suddenly started to empty. (Local legend, stoutly denied by the National Coal Board, has it that it emptied overnight.) Yet local people remember these times with affection — screeching about on dodgems and rollercoasters, going to gigs in the ballroom (the Beatles, the Who, Oasis), picnics by the lake on Sunday afternoons. In 1981, the estate was sold to John Broome, developer of Alton Towers, who hoped to create a spectacular water park on the site. But his plans did not proceed, and in 1985 the site was sold off to the Coal Board, mouldering for a further decade until acquired by local property company St Modwen.

St Modwen had an unusual proposition for the site — to turn it back into a garden of note, a spectacular showpiece that would become a leisure destination of national significance. Instead of a great house to visit, there would be a shopping village, a massive garden centre and a hotel, all helping to fund a £100 million regeneration scheme. It would be nothing less than the biggest garden restoration project in Europe.

They commissioned surveys and master plans from landscape architects Dominic Cole and Elizabeth Banks, who brought in plantsmen Piet Oudolf and Tom Stuart-Smith in a bid to reanimate the spirit of Trentham as a place at the leading edge of horticulture. They would recreate Barry's gardens, but with modern planting —

Capability Brown's great lake has been completely restored.

planting no less colourful, no less ambitious in scale; planting, in fact, that embodied challenge and innovation just as Fleming's had done.

But before planting of any kind could be contemplated, the site had to be reconstructed. It was a Herculean task. The paths, the banks, the fountains, the stonework — all needed rebuilding. Even the soil, it turned out, would have to be replaced — compacted clay exchanged with new topsoil, mushroom compost and endless lorry loads of horse manure. It required nothing less than a modern Paxton for the job. To Cole's mind, there was only one man up to the challenge: Michael Walker.

Michael's CV was impeccable. He had spent the last nine years as head gardener at Waddesdon Manor, the great Victorian garden of the Rothschild family, leased back to them by the National Trust. Since 1990, Lord Rothschild had spent some £60 million restoring the run-down garden to the apotheosis of Victorian splendour, rebuilding the palatial aviary, restoring Italianate parterres every bit as grand as Trentham's, and reclaiming the tradition of elaborate three-dimensional carpet bedding for which Waddesdon had been famous. While there was plenty of lavish Victorian pastiche, Michael also found himself working with artists as diverse as painter John Hubbard and fashion designer Oscar de la Renta to produce designs more in keeping with the late twentieth century. Most fascinating, for him, was to find a way of raising and installing the many thousands of plants required without recourse to a workforce of Victorian proportions, working with Cornish nursery Kernock Park Plants on a high-tech method of growing in pre-planned blocks that could be laid out like carpet tiles.

Before Waddesdon, Michael had restored Charles Barry's Italian Garden at Harewood House in Yorkshire. Here he had taken a scholarly, historical approach. 'Gardens are ephemeral, never created to be something for ever,' avers Michael. 'The right thing at the time seemed to be to restore the scheme we had the most amount of evidence for, and to give a Victorian bedding display with perennial planting around it. Then Lord Harewood commissioned *Orpheus*, a very modern sculpture, within that historic setting, and I felt maybe we should all have been braver; maybe we should have listened to those voices that said we should be really contemporary. Certainly, if I were there now I would do it differently.'

Trentham Gardens, then, offered an opportunity to revisit that conundrum — to understand the history and significance of the site (in all its many layers, not just its Victorian heyday), to intuit the spirit of place, but to find a way of expressing it in a more exciting and contemporary way. His first impression of Trentham had been dismal: 'the saddest garden I ever saw'. But he would be working with the best of the best in the field of landscape architecture and planting design, with an ample budget. And a mischievous part of his nature relished the idea of working

The lakeside walks are enlivened with ever-changing displays of art.

for a property developer – widely considered, like bankers, as the spawn of Satan. He arrived on site in February 2004; four weeks later he counted one hundred contractors working in the Italian Garden in a single day; by May 2004 the first stage was complete.

'We knew within days that we could just leave him to get on with it,' recalls Cole; 'that he'd make the decisions on site that would need to be made, and that those decisions would be the right ones. There are many head gardeners who are very good at growing things, but there are few that have the historical grasp that Michael has, his sensitivity to the details that matter, or his adeptness in organizing contractors to get exactly the result he requires. The thing that stands out about him is his sheer competence. Whatever problem you throw at him, there seems to be nothing he can't do.'

No doubt Michael Walker's resilience was formed in childhood. He was brought up in Belfast on the Antrim Road, known during the height of the Troubles as 'Murder Mile'. Michael insists it was a nice place to grow up, a middle-class area where Protestants and Catholics lived peaceably side by side. Nonetheless, as violence flared and more and more people moved from the city, the family hit hard times. Michael's father had inherited an estate agency, and Michael had always assumed he would follow him into the business – but no one was buying houses now. The local school declined from having two thousand pupils to fewer than three hundred. It made little difference to Michael, a reluctant student who contrived to fail every one of his GCSEs. Summoned to the careers office, he declared first that he wanted to join the mounted police, then that he would become a lighthouse keeper. Training for neither being conveniently to hand, he was sent off to enrol at Greenmount College for a one-year course in horticulture. College proved a revelation, and when a National Trust traineeship came up at Mount Stewart in County Down, he was eager. He was eighteen years old, and had found his path.

'I'd failed abysmally at school. I just had no interest – I couldn't focus on things. But gardening allowed me to wander off and be good at the things I like being good at.'

From Mount Stewart he was seconded to Powis and the maverick Jimmy Hancock, who was to become his father-in-law. Then came a short spell at Birmingham Botanical Gardens, before returning to the bosom of the Trust at Castle Drogo, Devon, where he became very good at cutting hedges. It was Jimmy who encouraged him to try for the position at Beningbrough Hall in 1986. Here, over six happy years, he learned his trade, before crossing into the private sector at Harewood House, charged with revitalizing a complex of gardens set, like Trentham's, in a Capability Brown park.

The Trentham project got off to a flying start. By early spring 2005, Michael had planted some seventy thousand perennials and tens of thousands of bulbs to furnish Tom Stuart-Smith's restored parterres. By 2007, Piet Oudolf's rivers of grass and Floral Labyrinth were also complete, creating the biggest perennial display in Europe, and attracting rave reviews from the gardening press.

Michael poses beneath a giant metalwork seedhead.

Yet somehow Trentham failed to establish itself as a destination garden in the way of Hidcote or Sissinghurst, and by 2008, when recession hit, there was some major rethinking to be done. During sweeping management changes Michael stepped forward to take responsibility not just for the garden but for the whole estate. To his mind, there was only one solution, desirable in both economic and landscape terms: to reunite the garden with the lakeside walks and surrounding parkland. This was deeply unpopular with locals, as these areas had previously been free to visit. But Michael rode out the flak, and paying visitor numbers soon started to grow, reaching half a million in 2015. 'Obviously I didn't like the hostile reaction, and there isn't a single project that I wouldn't do a little differently with hindsight, but on the whole I'm fairly gung-ho, and when you get to the end and it's all tidy, it feels fine.'

Since then, there have been more controversial decisions, as Michael embarked on an ambitious scheme to restore the parkland in time for Capability Brown's tercentenary in 2016. This involved felling over thirty thousand trees and introducing grazing over one hundred and twenty acres. To do it, he had to obtain permissions from a host of environmental quangos, no small test to his diplomatic skills — but not perhaps as gruelling as being constantly on hand to explain what was happening to furious tree-hugging visitors. Nevertheless, within four months of clear-felling in spring 2015, the dreary former timber plantation was already looking convincingly like a Brownian park.

'Being a head gardener is being an advocate for your garden. It's about negotiation, and persuading people to invest in you. With me, that's been about investing in new planting, or removing trees, or big restoration schemes — things that cost a significant amount of money. Often one needs to attract Lottery funding or some other kind of grant. But most important is to develop the relationship with owners or managers so that they are completely behind what you're doing.'

He followed this up by inviting Professor Nigel Dunnett, of nearby Sheffield University, to create some two miles of new gardens round the lakeshore, branching out from the wild flower meadows that have made his reputation to shady perennial plantings, groves of North American trees and shrubs, and a new wet woodland garden around one of the streams that feeds the lake. Not for Michael the usual boggy suspects — the gunneras and skunk cabbage, the hostas and primulas — too much of a cliché, he protests, too suburban. Instead he has in mind a lakeshore he once saw in Canada, covered in a sci-fi swarm of fly-eating pitcher plants (*Sarracenia purpurea*). 'It was freezing there in winter, so they should all be hardy in Staffordshire,' he says gleefully. You can imagine the consternation at the Gardens Trust at the prospect of carnivorous plants in a Capability Brown landscape.

Yet for all his delight in subverting expectations, Michael has become very much an establishment figure. In 2012 he was invited to join the National Trust Gardens panel, offering advice on all aspects of its gardens, from considering design changes to plant sourcing to everyday management and interpretation. In 2015 he was elevated to chairman — regrettably for only a few short months before, in a bureaucratic restructure inexplicable to many of the Trust's supporters, the expert panel was done away with in favour of a larger body covering architecture, archaeology and environment. The official line is that this aids joined-up thinking, and that there are in fact more gardens advisers, in more regions, from more diverse backgrounds, than before. But others maintain that the loss to the organization's gardeners is incalculable. Not only have they lost free access to many thousands of pounds' worth of consultancy with the leading experts in the field, but they had it mediated by someone who understood the practicalities of running a Trust garden and had actually done the job himself. Michael continues to serve on the new body, and is far too polite to articulate his disappointment.

In this position, and in his role as vice-president of the Professional Gardeners' Guild, Michael has had ample opportunity to consider how the role of head gardener has changed. It has become more corporate, he feels. There is less room for mavericks. Above all, he feels that were he to start again today, it would be much harder to achieve what he has. 'Coming from Northern Ireland with no ties over here, I was very free to move about to follow an opportunity, and could do so because accommodation was routinely part of the package. That's no longer the case today.'

He has considered moving on. There are many who would like to have him. 'But my girls are settled at local schools, and I'd like to finish what I've started here,' he says. He feels there is plenty of challenge still ahead: replanting the woodlands, reclaiming the wetlands destroyed by Fleming's river diversion and improving the degraded edges of Brown's lake, just for starters. Habitat restoration is an immediate concern. Continuing to reveal the full extent of the Brownian landscape is the work of a generation. And then the time will come to revisit Tom's and Piet's plantings — no garden should ever become a fossil.

Ask him if he sees himself as an innovator in the mould of Fleming and he'll say no. He's just a man who's good at getting things done. 'I'm satisfied that the garden is now self-sustaining, and that the balance of activities in the garden is sound, making a genuine contribution to the finances without being too destructive to the garden. I'm glad Trentham plays a major part in the community, that we still have a boat club and fishing on the lake, that we provide facilities for local schools and clubs. I'd like to see that side develop more, so that local people come to have a real sense of connection with the garden, and make use of it throughout the changing seasons.

'I am lucky to have supportive and imaginative employers. I have an excellent team, and I'm good at delegating. My job now is to get other people to deliver, so that I can have time to think, to step back and see how best to push Trentham forward.'

It's hard to imagine Michael ever resting on his laurels — it's just not in his nature to sit still. But more than that, he firmly believes that complacency is the death blow to creativity. 'It's good to have a job that pushes you: increasingly, my job requires me to understand things that I've never understood before.'

MISSION IMPOSSIBLE

MARTIN OGLE
Lowther Castle, Cumbria

'If you don't try, you don't know what talents you have . . .'

WHEN MARTIN OGLE has had a tough day at work he goes home, gets on his mountain bike, and heads for the Lakeland fells. Here, swooping high above Ullswater, or spinning down some dizzy track towards Windermere, at one with wind and water, he forgets everything else, high on the speed, the control, the precarious balance, the needling sense of danger. When he comes home, muddy and exhausted, his body aches but his mind is free. Then he'll fall into bed, ready to rise at first light, because the days are never long enough for all that Martin has to do. For the truth is, every day is a tough day for Martin Ogle. And anyone less determined, less resilient, less courageous, would have got on his bike and pedalled off long ago.

Ask him why he doesn't give up, and he'll say he enjoys a challenge. The steeper the slope, the more vertiginous the drop, the more he likes it. If he rides the same track more than twice in a month, he'll get bored, and won't return till it's glassy with snow and ice. What's life, he asks, if you don't push yourself? This is a man who has swum with sharks, trekked through jungles and been dropped from a helicopter to ride a bike straight down the New Zealand Remarkables mountain range. Clearly, he doesn't scare easily. Yet who in their right mind would not be daunted by the test of nerve that was handed to Martin — to take charge of the biggest garden renovation project in the UK, but with no job security, no budget and no staff whatsoever?

Scroll back twenty years. When Martin was a boy, he would ride out into the hills from his Penrith home and, climbing above Ullswater, a fairytale Gothic castle would appear high on the limestone ridge above the River Lowther. A roofless ruin smothered in ivy, it seemed lost in the slumber of centuries.

In reality Lowther Castle is not so old. It was begun in 1806 by Cumbrian architect Robert Smirke, his first major commission. Later Smirke would design the sober British Museum, but this was a young man's fancy, rejoicing in every extravagance of the Gothic Revival, all turrets and battlements and cathedral-scale lancet windows, rising improbably from a serene expanse of lawn.

The site had been occupied since at least the twelfth century, and the first recorded gardens set out in the 1690s by Sir John Lowther — an elaborate pattern of lawns, formal walks, fruit and vegetables, bounded by a dramatic terrace dangling on the garden's edge, offering panoramic views of the surrounding hills. That terrace still survives, the views as epic as ever.

Successive earls of Lonsdale added to the garden, but the baroque framework was still more or less intact in 1882, when the Fifth Earl inherited. Aided by fashionable designer Thomas Mawson, he promptly set about embellishing the scene, squeezing in a series of some twenty pleasure gardens decorated with fountains and pavilions and curious stone cairns.

Hugh Lowther, popularly known as the Yellow Earl (it was his favourite colour), was a spectacularly energetic spendthrift who liked fast cars, pretty actresses, hunting and sport. He founded the Automobile Association (branded yellow to this day), was a director of Arsenal Football Club (who still play away in yellow), and instituted the Lonsdale Belt in boxing. With no child to whom to bequeath his substantial fortune, he made it his mission to spend the lot. His excesses were legendary, and his exploits — as a circus rider, buffalo hunter, Arctic explorer and Lothario — kept Edwardian high society entertained for years. His cigar bill alone, Martin reports with a certain awe, came to £4,000 a year — about £100,000 in today's money. By 1937, the coffers were finally bare, and Lowther Castle was abandoned. In 1942 the army requisitioned the site for testing a top secret anti-tank weapon, and the seventeenth-century terraces were finally obliterated under tons of concrete.

The Yellow Earl died in 1944, leaving colossal debts. To clear them, the castle was stripped of its contents; even the potted bonsai trees adorning the Japanese Garden were auctioned off. In 1957 the roof was ripped off, the ruin filled with pig pens, and the concreted south lawns, once the playground of European royalty, were turned over to chicken-farming. The remainder was planted over with a cash crop of spruce.

And so it remained, for over fifty dismal years, until in 2008 a trust was formed with the intention of rescuing the castle and opening the gardens as

PAGES 204–205 *Where once there were* parterrres de broderie, *now is a sea of wild carrot.*
OPPOSITE *Following the Dissolution of the Monasteries, stone from nearby Shap Abbey was raided for Lowther. These steps are put together from sections of columns, producing their curious 'love-heart' effect.*

a visitor attraction. Among the experts brought in to advise was landscape architect and historian Dominic Cole. He suggested uncovering the bones of the seventeenth-century garden once more, but that rather than recreating a period garden, they should work within the pattern of the historic layout to create a new garden for a new century. Two important steps must follow. This new garden would need a master plan — and who better then Dan Pearson to provide it? And an outstanding head gardener must be engaged to oversee the work. Cole drew up a job specification. He based it, in every particular, on Michael Walker.

'I wouldn't call myself reckless, but I'm always looking for a challenge: I want to push myself.'

Who would have thought that a long-familiar landmark could suddenly alter the course of your life? Having trained as a gardener (an apprenticeship at an old-fashioned estate garden followed by six years at a tree nursery), Martin couldn't wait to get away. He travelled widely throughout his twenties, gardening where he could — raising London planes in Western Australia and in New Zealand tending football pitches in Queenstown and pruning apples in Hawkes Bay. 'The thing about travelling is that it made me fully aware of where I live, here in the Lakes, and I never really appreciated that until I'd been away. When I came back I knew this was where I really wanted to be.'

But jobs in rural Cumbria are hard to come by, and he was on the point of setting off adventuring in Canada. Now a position on a high-profile project, working with some of the top names in gardening, was being offered right in his back yard. For Martin, it was almost too good to be true. And indeed it was: when the head gardener's job was finally advertised, he didn't get it. But encouraged to apply again, this time as one of two supporting gardeners, he was appointed to Lowther in March 2012.

By this time, contractors had been busy felling over two thousand trees, clearing away the concrete and reinstating the original levels. Work was underway to make the tottering castle walls safe, and the cleaned-up entrance courtyard now offered a shop and a rather good cafe. After years of mud and destruction, it was time to begin creating, to start putting Pearson's plan into action. These were exciting times. But within months of Martin's arrival, the main contractors on the project went into administration. Visitors could hardly be admitted while the ruin was still dangerous, so in order to complete the consolidation, all funding was commandeered from the garden. Late in 2012, his colleague was made redundant. Days later, the head gardener resigned. By February 2013, Martin was there on his own. The head gardener's job was his if he was happy

Once the roof was stripped off in 1957, the castle soon fell into ruin.

to stay: the aim of turning 130 derelict acres into a national garden attraction remained unaltered, but he would have to achieve it with no budget at all, and entirely by himself.

'You could class it as an impossible situation,' says Martin mildly. 'But the way I looked at it was, if you've been asked to achieve something with no staff and no budget, and if you can implement even a little bit of change, then that's worth some acknowledgement. I didn't have a family to support: I was at a time in my life where I could afford to give it a go. At the end of the day, if it didn't work, I could walk away with my head held high and say, "At least I tried." It would be no fault of mine if it failed; I would do my best with the resources I was given.

'I knew this opportunity was one I had to grasp with both hands. I had to sit down with the trustees right away and come up with some kind of plan.'

It is difficult to know how to waken a Sleeping Beauty. Too thick a tangle of weed and thorn around her, and her loveliness is occluded. But bring her too abruptly into the light and her mystery is shattered, all magic gone. Some gardens get it right, as at Ninfa, near Rome. Others don't: many who adored The Lost Gardens of Heligan in Cornwall in their early, wilderness days, now complain they have been over-restored.

This was the conundrum Martin had to address – how to acknowledge the garden's past grandeur, and yet respect what the garden had become – a magical place of crepuscular glades and tumbledown summer houses, where leaves whispered in long-abandoned pools, and fat cushions of moss had spread over rocks and stonework, and the ghostly arteries of once grand avenues lingered among the ferns.

Happily, he had a firm steer in Dan Pearson's master plan. Ever sensitive to the spirit of place, Pearson proposed to create two new garden areas — a parterre in front of the south facade, and a Ninfa-style garden within the castle walls. But much of the rest would remain 'lost', evocative shadows of what had been, where a new ecology now thrived, as Pearson put it, 'amid ancient trees, Roman columns and Egyptian baths'.

Martin's first decision as head gardener was, controversially, to stand down the hack-and-slash services of the local probation service, and to set about delicately digging out the remainder of the chain of Edwardian gardens buried in the western part of the garden. 'The idea was not to put them back to how they were, but to preserve that lost and romantic feeling the gardens had. Some we will recreate, such as a new version of the Rose Garden, but some, such as the Japanese and Sweet Scented Gardens, we will just keep as ruins. So we'll leave the herb robert trailing over the water features, and the silent dead ponds, and try and get people to engage with what was here.'

This approach has paid dividends. In the once-celebrated Rock Garden, Dan had suggested building a platform over the garden and viewing it from above. Martin preferred patiently to uncover the original network of paths and, aided by a doughty team of volunteers, to weed through over and over again by hand. 'The more we've cultivated the soil, the more we've exposed seeds, so that now all these plants are popping up,' he says. These include snowdrops, primulas, orchids, wild ginger, colchicums, saxifrages and, every spring, a mass of *Trillium chloropetalum*. To these have been added donations of hellebores, dicentras, giant cowslips and shuttlecock ferns. Already he has the makings of a successful woodland garden.

Researching the Japanese Garden, laid out in 1902–3, Martin found an old photo which showed bonsai trees in pots, two tea-houses, and a flock of stags and storks in bronze. 'It was really, really fussy. It's much more beautiful as it is now.' There's something somehow truer to the spirit of Japan in the simple arrangement

FROM LEFT TO RIGHT *In the Rock Garden, the original paths have been unearthed, twisting and twining between the beds. One of seven stone cairns discovered in the Sweet Scented Garden. An ancient stone seat invites a pause for reflection.* ·

of moss-quilted rocks, especially in the winter, when the leaves die back and they are lit by a low, glancing sun. Beyond that, lies the Sweet Scented Garden (a fashionable trope in Edwardian gardens), where visitors would linger in arbours clad with honeysuckle, listening to the water splash from seven stone cairns. And somewhere nearby there was a topiary garden, but no one is entirely sure where.

The highlight of the Edwardian ensemble was probably the Rose Garden — now a manageable area of open lawn. Here, one day, Martin hopes to make a new rose garden around the remains of the old central fountain. Last comes the site of the Iris Garden — a scatter of rocks between tall pillars of spruce where herons nest. It comes as a shock to remember the whole garden looked like this only a few short years ago.

Critical to this achievement are Lowther's volunteers. Twice a week, Martin emails some forty willing souls, and generally over half of them turn up. Many, like him, have known the castle since childhood, and feel a deep sense of connection with it. They can turn their hands to most things: weeding, strimming, planting, propagating. With no budget to speak of, almost everything is grown from seeds and cuttings, and they also run a plant stall, selling off anything that can't be used in the garden to raise money for Dan's specified plants. If Martin feels the disjunction between the labour that goes into raising these pennies and the fee structure of world-famous garden designers (not to mention the £9 million of initial project funding), he gives nothing away.

Diplomacy is a new skill he's had to learn — when your workforce is unpaid, you can't just boss them around. 'Prior to coming here, I'd never had a management role — so I had to pick it up very, very quickly,' he says. 'Some volunteers have been here from the beginning so they've seen the place change with me. They see the challenges that are put on me and they want to help; I think they have a respect for what I've achieved. And I respect them for the love they obviously have for the place, and the work and commitment they put in. You get to know their characters, what they like doing, how best to deploy them around the garden. You get the odd disaster: one volunteer carefully pulled up all the wild ginger. But if you have plenty of people and you can keep their spirits high — supply cake at lunchtime and chat about what's going on in their own gardens — it's amazing how time passes, and how much we can get done.'

There's a Catch-22 here that's plain for all to see. Without any staff, you can't create a garden worth looking at. And until there's a garden worth looking at, there won't be the visitors to fund the staff.

'I won't lie, 2013 was a tough year,' admits Martin grudgingly (he's not given to moaning), though he was at last permitted an apprentice — scarcely a major investment at a measly £2.65 an hour. Then, in 2014, he managed to secure a part-time position for one of his volunteers, an experienced plantswoman, to oversee the new Dan Pearson plantings.

First up was a new parterre in front of the castle, a grid formation of yew hedging and perennial planting intended to suggest the texture of a threadbare tapestry, an intricate matrix of irises, salvias, astrantias and gillenias, with sanguisorba, veronicastrum and thalictrum lending height. It's a little more threadbare, perhaps, than Pearson intended, as they couldn't afford anything

Years of neglect have made a haven for wildlife. Great crested newts thrive in Jack Croft's Pond among the rushes and flag iris, carefully cleared to cause minimum disturbance.

like the number of plants specified and grew the lion's share themselves, but by massing them in patches, the essential feel of an embroidered carpet has already been achieved.

Now it was time to start on the heart of Pearson's new plan — a garden blossoming within the ruined walls, with climbers clambering through the Gothic windows and small trees seeming to sprout spontaneously from the floors, with pools of shady perennials cascading around their feet — a deeply romantic garden that would evoke all the magic of a lost, enchanted castle — a kind of Ninfa of the North. Though Martin had never been to Ninfa, he could see it clearly in his mind's eye.

'I spent a lot of time trying to visualize it. What you have on paper and in your head is a fantasy, and there are moments when you wonder how you are going to make it work, when you don't doubt yourself, exactly, but you have a lot of questions. The garden stands at six hundred feet, and the winters are cold and long. We thought it would be sheltered within the walls, but it's not — the wind blasts straight through. I love Dan's plant palette — the magnolias and cornus, the schizophragmas and ampelopsis, but we don't know how much of it will survive this far north.' One things is sure, if they can survive, Martin will make sure they do. 'You'll always figure out a way of getting to your goal if you work hard enough and apply what you've learned in the past,' insists Martin. 'You'll always get there in the end.'

'My mantra is Find a Way. If you speak to my friends or colleagues they'll tell you I'm quite stubborn. There's always a way if you look hard enough.'

Martin has had to work hard — talking, blogging, tweeting — to persuade visitors more accustomed to neat herbaceous borders that this apparently dishevelled planting will grow into grace and beauty and, just as importantly, to put their hands in their pockets to sponsor the larger plants needed for the scheme. 'Helping people to identify with the garden is an essential part of the project,' says Martin, 'and of course the more change they can see, the more it encourages them to get involved. Lowther needs to be a gem within the local community, something we can all be proud of. We want it to become a notable garden destination for the north of England.'

There have already been some hugely successful community projects. Replanting the orchard, for example, has become a focus for sharing grafting techniques and other orchard skills. And in October 2012, 612 volunteers broke the world record for bulb planting, putting in 106,652 *Narcissus poeticus* bulbs in just three back-breaking but convivial hours. These bulbs now mark out the Yellow Earl's *patte d'oie* that dominates the eastern side of the garden —

three converging avenues once delineated by elaborate carpet bedding. It gives you some idea, suggests Martin, of how the original plantings would have felt, but it's another example of inspired updating – infinitely more joyful, more appropriate to the setting, and mercifully maintenance free.

Standing at the fulcrum of the *patte d'oie*, looking out over the broad central lawns with their fringe of wild flowers, the tidy blocks of trees, the colourful new parterre, it is clear what a vast amount has been achieved. Turn around, though, and you see just how much is left to do. A rusting stairway leads up to a long, iris-choked pond, overlooked by a rustic summer house sagging beneath a Niagara of ivy. Beyond is all wild woodland. You can see the line of an old avenue of copper beeches, and detect scraps of pathway from the remains of stone edgings, but it will be decades before any of these are dug out. Then there are the shelter belts to think about, and the estate woodland to be got back into shape. He'd like to make a new productive garden, perhaps in the old kitchen range. He'd like to restore the once splendid pinetum. 'I think', says Martin drily, 'there's probably enough to keep me going for the rest of my life.'

He's trying to take, he says with only the faintest flicker of a smile, a Chinese outlook – planning for the next five hundred years. But at just thirty-six he has a long career ahead of him. Isn't he a bit young to have fixed on his life's work?

'It's a job to see my career out for sure. But I can't see myself doing anything else right now,' says Martin. 'There's such a lot to achieve here – it's exciting, unique – completely different from any National Trust-type property. I've had amazing opportunities: working on a Dan Pearson plan isn't the kind of thing you do every day. I hope he's proud of it: it would be great to reconnect with him, to see if it's all going as he imagined. But the best thing is, you're constantly learning, every single day – things are always changing and you need to adapt,

Martin is excited to get to work on the garden in the heart of the ruins.

to learn new methods. It is very challenging — I'm not going to deny that — but it is a challenge I'm enjoying.'

Nonetheless, there must surely be days when he gets discouraged, when the task seems too enormous, when it's just all too much? Even nature sometimes seems against him. Enormous storms in 2013 laid waste 400-year-old veteran trees, while the Christmas storms of 2015 that decimated Cumbria smashed the ancient yew avenue, swept away paths and took out the monumental Grand Fir which stood at the highest point in the garden, a landmark tree that could be seen for miles around.

'I'm not going to lie. There are times I think, do I really want to be doing this? But reading the history of the gardens you see people's names repeated — you want to be part of that, you want your name to be in the story.'

'Yes, there are down days when you're struggling just to stand still — where you're struggling to complete a job or there's no money for something essential or no staff. But it's part of my job, finding ways to deal with those things. You just get on and do it.'

Tenacity is in the genes. His dad is a grafter, as was his grandad too. 'It is rare to see my dad stopped; he'll just keep beavering away at something till it's done,' says Martin. 'And I always remember my grandad gardening till late in the evening. He was an engineer for North West Water, and he would be out ten, twelve hours a day at work, come home and have his tea, and then he'd get out into the garden.' It was his grandad who taught him to garden, chasing the eight-year-old Martin up a ladder to subdue a rampant Virginia creeper, teaching him to use edging shears, grow veg and prune the roses.

The Ogles, then, are men of relentless energy. But Martin's problem is that the more he does, the more he has to do. For every new piece of garden he brings under cultivation then requires a higher level of care. 'Staffing is a huge, huge mountain. And as the garden develops, every week, every day, every hour, more of my time is taken up with planning and organization, so I just can't be out on the mower all day long. At the minute, we're on the cusp of managing but if we stick to the plan, we're going to need at least one more person full-time next year.'

Maybe, he concedes, he's his own worst enemy, working every day until he drops. 'Maybe if I didn't do as much, it would be more obvious that more staff are needed. It's down to my ambitious nature, that I want to see things happen, I want to see things work. In the end, it's my reputation and my name against it, so I guess I'll do whatever I have to do to achieve those goals. I want to stand back in ten, fifteen years' time and be proud of what's been done. And I want people

He can see a whole lifetime's work ahead at Lowther.

to be proud of me. I want the trustees to stand by my side and say, "It's down to this lad, he's done a great job." I think that will happen.'

You find you believe it too. For there's no boast or bombast in this assertion, just a quiet, implacable determination. You might as well argue with the steady Cumbrian rain. 'It's not that I want applause,' Martin continues, suddenly uncomfortable. 'I'm like my mum, quite a shy person, someone who'd rather stay in the background. But I do have confidence in myself, not just as a gardener but as a person. I thrive on personal goals and personal achievements, and if you want to achieve something, whatever it is, you have to have belief in yourself; it's impossible without.

'Everything is achievable — you've just to find a way of doing it. And if *you* can't find it, there are always people who will help you, not just in the horticultural world, but in life generally. To do my job, I have to believe it can be achieved.'

Sometimes that might look like folly. 'A guy came up to me the other day and said, "If they offer you redundancy, mate, take it and run."' Martin shrugs. 'I wasn't angry. I just didn't listen. Because the next person who comes along will be full

of praise and wish you all the best for the future, so those are the comments I choose to feed on. Some people can be fired up by negative feedback, but I just ignore it.

'I hope I don't come across as a huge ego – I know how lucky I am to be here. There are probably a lot of people who hate going to work in the morning, but I still enjoy coming here every day. I enjoy the people I work with; I enjoy speaking to people about what we're doing. I never relax. If it's the weekend, I'll be out on my bike – you'll never catch me sitting about unless it's dark and I can't be outside. I want to experience as much as I can in everything I do; whether it's being out in the landscape or working here in the garden, I want to get the most out of life.'

Studied dereliction: the water is now clear, and a view has been opened into the garden.

PARTNERS IN PERFECTIONISM

JIM BUCKLAND & SARAH WAIN
West Dean Gardens, West Sussex

'It has been a blessed position. We've been able to demonstrate what we can do, and we've been given the wherewithal to do it. We've been able to make our mark.'

SO WHO'S THE HEAD GARDENER? Is it Jim or is it Sarah? His title is Gardens Manager, so, technically, he's the boss. But Sarah is Gardens Supervisor, which is what a head gardener does. He is the bigger picture man. She is the expert grower. He does the fruit; she does the veg. She is good at colour and design and propagation. He is good at strategy. The long and the short of it is that they've worked together for over twenty-five years, as indivisible as Bill and Ben, Wallace & Gromit, or 'Fred Astaire and Ginger Rogers', suggests Jim. Sarah stifles a snort. They share the head gardener's office at West Dean Gardens in Sussex. (And while it's Jim's name that appears on the door, the sunshine-yellow walls are Sarah's choice.) They have desks at opposite ends of the room. It is very neat, not at all cosy. Lots of lists. No kettle. Emphatically a place of work. Isn't it hard, working with your spouse, being together day and night?

'Not a bit of it,' says Sarah, brightly. 'I come from Australian farming stock, where it's the norm for married couples, for whole families, to work together year in, year out. No one thinks anything of it. My parents lived and worked together, so I didn't think it was unusual at all. Besides,' she continues, deadpan, 'West Dean is a very large garden.'

Jim chuckles. This is clearly a familiar routine, tossing the ball to and fro, to and fro. They would find it impossible now, they agree, to work without each other. Even their speech is intertwined. Listening to them is like listening to a tune on the piano: the left and the right hand playing together create the melody. If you were to transcribe their speech in two different colours, you'd see two ribbons looping around each other. Jim is the more voluble, often speaking in long sentences which trail away, as if waiting for Sarah to complete them.

She doesn't. She's shorter, pithier, supplying the decisive chord at the right moment, quiet but firm, not interrupting; rather anchoring the virtuoso swoops and trills of the upper stave.

'It's been fantastic for us because we do fundamentally respect each other and enjoy each other's company. The place would not be as good if Sarah wasn't here.'

Not all, of course, is perfect harmony. She's not above telling him off when she thinks he's over-critical or rude, and staff have been known to creep quietly by when the noise of a mighty ding-dong is ringing from the potting shed. 'We're both feisty people. We'll have a good barney,' offers Sarah. 'But we never let the sun go down on our wrath,' pipes Jim, making a simpering face.

BELOW, LEFT AND RIGHT *In the office. Sarah's comprehensive lists are the key to good organization at West Dean.*

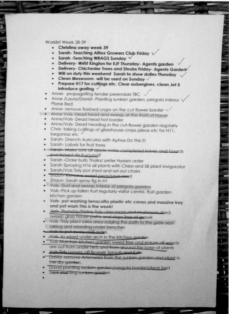

They laugh a lot. Jim clearly enjoys a spot of clowning, and there's a level at which they don't take themselves too seriously. It's not hard, for instance, to tempt them out into the yard for an impromptu game of conkers. Work, however, is deadly serious. Running a garden the size and complexity of West Dean takes diligence, skill and supreme organization. Their aim, within the historic nineteenth-century setting, is to demonstrate the very highest standards in horticulture. 'West Dean was set up to be a centre of excellence for the arts and crafts,' explains Jim. (It was endowed as an arts foundation in 1964.) 'And we want the garden to do the same.'

———⬦———

West Dean House, a Gothic Revival pile gloriously set in the South Downs National Park near Chichester, was home to Edward James (1907–84), an early devotee of surrealism who championed Salvador Dalí and René Magritte and famously created a surrealist garden in the depths of the Mexican jungle. Though he was born and buried at West Dean (his grave lies in the arboretum), his other ventures clearly distracted him from the garden, which, despite some fine features (such as the nearly 100-metre-long pergola by Harold Peto), was in a poor state by the time of his death.

PAGES 224–225 *West Dean's nineteenth-century glasshouses are once again objects of horticultural splendour.*
BELOW *A ventilation grille in one of the glasshouses.*

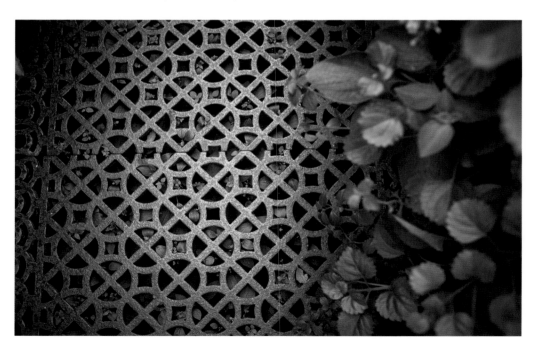

Back in 1995, virtually nobody grew chillies, though they had been popular in the nineteenth century.

The 1987 storm added to its woes, so that by the time Jim Buckland arrived on the scene in 1991, the garden was, in his words, 'pretty shite'. Jim found a landscape of some ninety acres comprising a somewhat amorphous Arts and Crafts garden set around with parkland, a battered arboretum and a ruined walled garden. Here he discovered a splintered but still stupendous range of Foster and Pearson glasshouses and all the decaying infrastructure of a top-flight Victorian kitchen garden. It was irresistible. This, he felt, could be the focus of a major restoration project that would put West Dean on the map. But first he needed Sarah on board. They had been working together at a Hampshire estate for the last three years, but he had applied for the head gardener post as an individual, and there was some initial resistance to hiring a working couple. Once the trustees had interviewed Sarah, however, there was no further argument. Jim started work in April 1991, Sarah joined him three months later, and together they began the work of turning West Dean Gardens into a national treasure, a byword for the flawless cultivation of fruit and vegetables, especially under glass.

In 1987, garden historian Peter Thoday and gardener Harry Dodson had set about reanimating a run-down walled garden for a BBC Two television series, *The Victorian Kitchen Garden*. The programme caught the national imagination, and none

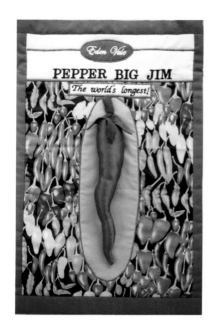

Pride of place in the office goes to this richly embroidered tribute to Jim's prowess.

were more avid viewers than Jim and Sarah, newly returned from five years in Australia.

'We *loved* that programme,' says Sarah. Indeed, Jim can still hum the theme tune. 'It was a revelation,' he continues, 'the complexity, the diversity, the sheer ingenuity of it. 'And it *worked*,' Sarah chips in. 'It was just tremendous horticulture, and that's what we wanted to aspire to. We hadn't worked in fruit and veg till that point, but we liked it, we'd both grown it as teenagers, and so it became our focus.'

The West Dean project wasn't just about restoring the glasshouses and frames, though that was done by 1994 (and now, after a quarter of a century, needs doing again – the maintenance is terrifying), but about recreating the approach to growing that obtained during the garden's glory years (roughly from the 1890s to 1912) – the diversity of produce, the skill that went into cheating the seasons, and above all a commitment to doing everything as well as it could possibly be done. Attention to detail was everything: no effort was spared in pursuit of what nineteenth-century garden writer and designer John Claudius Loudon called 'polish'. This was a time when a top head gardener such as James Barnes of Bicton Park in Devon would think nothing of keeping an apprentice busy for weeks on end simply painting string green. The kitchen garden should be not only efficient, not only munificently productive, but beautiful.

And so it is. Thirteen glasshouses, twinkling and scrubbed, burgeon with chillies and tomatoes, plump pink peaches and bloomy bunches of perfect grapes, not to mention a scintillating display of orchids and exotics in the authentic nineteenth-century manner. Frames are stuffed with seedlings, cuttings and cut-and come-again salads, with fragrant herbs and pots of pelargoniums. Dahlias strut magnificently in the cutting beds (no droopy heads here), backed by a tunnel of pears, and carefully labelled vegetables march in orderly rows across perfectly hoed, weedless soil. Ranged around the walls are perennial crops – asparagus, artichokes, gooseberries and rhubarb. Old water carriers and rollers lend a pleasantly antique air, yet there's some innovative horticulture going on here – not just trying new varieties (for some of the historic ones, in Sarah's view, are wildly overrated and were justly superseded), but testing new cultural techniques – new ways to grow today's popular baby leaf and stir-fry greens more intensively, and to keep every inch of garden producing at full tilt, without long gaps or wasted space.

There's a precision, an attention to detail, that seems to belong to another age — the way the wonderful textures of cabbages, veiny or frilly or glossed with a silver sheen, are set off by a mulch of bark chip; the blanching pots so carefully placed on the endives; unruly raspberries all neatly tied in with trim and tidy knots. In the fruit garden, heritage apples and pears have been coaxed into all manner of wondrous shapes, and the paths are lined with pristine zigzag hedges in imitation of crinkle-crankle walls. Everything is immaculate — the gravel raked, the paths weed-free; even the hoses are curled up in perfect circles and the watering cans lined up in military rows.

Their rigour is legendary: there's a right and a wrong way to do everything, from pricking out to hanging up the tools. And these exacting standards are maintained by eagle-eyed vigilance (Jim) and a highly tuned system of spreadsheets, diaries and colour-coded to-do lists (Sarah). 'I blame my German antecedents,' sighs Sarah, who admits she likes nothing better than crossing off a task in fat red pencil.

'Fruit and vegetables were fashionable when I started out in horticulture because we were all into self-sufficiency. Now they're flavour of the month again. But there's always a hard core of kitchen gardeners, because we all need to eat.'

'We talk about our horticultural year in weeks. It's all charted on spreadsheets and everything we do is recorded in a diary so we can make comparisons and adjustments year to year. It gives us a framework and allows us to project ahead. We bag up all our seed according to weeks, so you can just pick up your "week two" bag or your "week five" bag and off you go.'

If it all seems a bit anal, Jim isn't apologizing. 'We like order. The devil really is in the detail, especially under glass. There are so many small jobs which in themselves don't seem that significant, but if we are respected for what we do, that's because we identify all those jobs and do them in a timely fashion. A hell of a lot of horticulture is just good housekeeping: it doesn't big it up very much, but there it is.' Downplay it as he might, it's an approach that has paid off: in 2012 both gardeners were recognized by the horticultural establishment with prestigious awards, Jim being appointed one of the elite one hundred RHS Associates of Honour, while Sarah received both the Professional Gardeners' Guild Loyal Service Award and the Chartered Institute of Horticulture's Horticulture Award, held by no more than fifty people at a time.

<hr />

What are the qualities, then, that make an outstanding gardener?

'Vision,' says Sarah. That's Jim's forte — being able to picture what things will look like in five or ten or twenty years' time. Then there are all the skills of nurture, at which Sarah excels. But most important of all, they agree, is to be a good observer. His best lesson ever, Jim maintains, came from his early days at Capel Manor College. 'Our teacher, Mrs Roberts, always said, "If you're going to be a good gardener, you have to look, to respond, and think about what you're looking at."'

The decorative quality of well-grown cabbages is beyond doubt.
FROM LEFT TO RIGHT *'January King 3'; 'Red Jewel' F1 hybrid;'Ormskirk'.*

This spectacularly fan-trained fig is an example of Jim's mastery of the art of training fruit trees.

'And in Australia I was getting the same thing,' adds Sarah. '"Observation is Education" was the mantra there.'

Sarah studied horticultural science in Melbourne, before spending three years at Kew as assistant gardener in charge of the Australian collection. It was here, in 1980, she met Jim, then a student on the diploma course. He had been interested in growing since his teenage years, when he would putter about on his Honda 50 gathering up bracken or rotten vegetables for his compost heap. He also, Sarah announces in a stage whisper, once famously filled up his father's Mini with manure. When Sarah returned to Australia to take up a job at a local council nursery, her compost-coddling suitor followed in hot pursuit, hot being the operative word, for pale-skinned plantaholic Sarah had always loathed the 'toxic' Australian climate she'd grown up with. Five years later, the pair returned gratefully to soggy English summers.

Rainy British weather may well be, as Sarah claims, the best in the world for growing plants. It is not, however, ideal for the jolly days out for which West Dean Gardens have become famous. When Jim and Sarah staged Britain's first ever Chilli Fiesta in 1995, the idea was entirely novel. It was conceived as a fundraiser to attract more visitors to the garden and as a way, as they saw it, of repaying the investment both of money and of confidence that had been placed in them. (Huge sums were pouring not just into the restoration itself, but into developing a whole business infrastructure of visitor centre, cafe and shop to support it.) In those days the chilli was barely grown in Britain — though it had been well known in Victorian times — and Sarah had to scour the globe for varieties. But from the first, the festival was a hit. Expecting perhaps five hundred people, they were astonished when five times that number turned up. 'The original idea was that it should feel like an extended church fête, a bit homespun and cosy,' says Jim, 'and it certainly was that.' Chilli shows were followed by celebrations of apples, tomatoes, squashes and herbs, and soon they were holding five shows a year (on top of the day jobs) and attracting copycats worldwide. By the twentieth anniversary Chilli Fiesta in 2015, there were salsa bands, fireworks, camping and glamping, and twenty-two thousand people pouring in over three action-packed days. But Jim and Sarah had had enough.

'I don't think you can manage a large, complex garden creatively without knowing it intimately. There's a macrocosmic and a microcosmic element to it, and the two are equally important.'

'It was fun doing it . . .'
'. . . for the first ten years . . .'
'. . . and then it became too boring, too demanding, and it got in the way of the garden.'
'And we couldn't bring anything new to it,' interjects Sarah. 'We didn't have the spark to . . .'
'We were exhausted . . .'
'. . . well, my brain was . . .'
'We thought if it was going to go forward . . .'
'. . . someone else needed to take it on.'

These days someone else does the admin, though Jim still does all the site management — putting up and taking down tents and bridges, sorting out access and car parks and the signage, while Sarah prepares a punishing schedule of talks and demonstrations. They are both seasoned performers, easy and humorous yet commanding on stage. When Sarah lays down a feeding regime for your tomatoes, you listen, take note and do as you are told. Paradoxically, they have now begun to worry that the shows they pioneered have become too big, that too many of their visitors come specially for the events. 'All you need is a year like 2012 with sixteen inches of rain in six weeks and you're scuppered,' frets Sarah. 'It's not a secure way to build financial stability.'

'As an educational charity, we don't have to make massive profits,' explains Jim, 'but we've always seen it as part of our job to ensure that the garden breaks even and, broadly speaking, we've achieved that. We've been happy to have a public face because it enables us to go on improving the garden.' They write and lecture and chat on radio; they've had series in the gardening glossies and slots on TV. Just as there are writers'

writers who never appear on supermarket bookshelves but are lauded by their peers, it seems there are gardeners' gardeners: while they may not have the TV exposure of Alan Titchmarsh or Carol Klein, for example, Buckland and Wain were mentioned repeatedly and with unreserved admiration by many other head gardeners in this book.

'Head gardener', however, is a title Jim has dispensed with. 'It's a crap description of what you do. You're managing a staff of ten, plus around forty volunteers, and you're responsible for everything. We set the business centre up. We built the car park. We made the new entrances. We manage the plant sales. We drove all that, so we've been responsible really for creating the gardens as a viable public offering. It's a very different job from being a head gardener with a family, working on your own. Having said that, we've just planted seventy-six thousand bulbs and I've personally made the hole for a couple of thousand of them. You might say it's not a good use of my time, but I believe it is. I don't think you can manage a large, complex garden creatively without knowing it intimately. There's a macrocosmic and a microcosmic element to it, and the two are equally important.'

'This is supposed to be a nation of gardeners. But I think it's a questionable statement. You only have to get on a train and look into people's gardens: you don't go yahoo! very often do you?'

Indeed. But is his job really any more demanding than that of the Victorian head gardener, required to be florist, botanist, chemist and meteorologist, surveyor, designer and draughtsman, also haulage contractor, tool-maker and heating engineer? Does working with an educational foundation require any more delicate diplomatic skills than negotiating the competing demands of employer, housekeeper and cook

– often in more than one establishment? It is perhaps slightly more complicated to plan work when the lion's share of your workforce is voluntary. 'We give them a hundred lines when they don't turn up,' jokes Jim, not altogether blithely, and you sense he'd rather like to, just in the way James Barnes at Bicton would levy fines on his workers for turning up in a dirty shirt (rule one; fine threepence) or for 'leaving a job unfinished, in an unworkmanlike manner' (rule eleven; threepence again). The largest fine, a whole shilling, was for leaving something dangerous around the furnaces, or – cannily – for 'in any way mutilating or defacing the above Rules'.[1]

Sarah, of course, has everything perfectly under control, factoring in a 60 to 70 per cent take-up rate each week. Her admiration for her crew is unfeigned, and their skills are impressive – specialist expertise in machine maintenance, welding and chainsaw operation as well as fruit management and general horticultural duties. They seem to welcome the garden's strict regime without demur, regarding it as a benchmark, a way of learning how to do things properly. Some are career changers, drawn to West Dean by the wide range of horticultural disciplines on offer – glasshouse management and fruit and vegetable cultivation, of course, but also propagation, flower border maintenance, the management of two national collections of trees (horse chestnuts and tulip trees), even the art of achieving a pristine lawn.

---

1 From a sheet entitled 'Rules and Regulations of the Plant Department in Bicton Gardens, Sept. 26th, 1842'.

A display of squashes exhibits their extraordinary variety of colour, shape and size. FROM LEFT, *in the bowl, spiky* Cucumis zambianus, Melothria scabra *and* Cucumis metuliferus, *with, to right of bowl,* Cucumis dipsaceus. *The colour-changing winter variety 'Festival'. A new white scallop squash, as yet unnamed.*

Others are locals who have been pitching up for decades, and many have become good friends.

———✦———

There's a picture of the garden team at Wrest Park in Bedfordshire, published in the *Gardeners' Chronicle* in 1903, which notes that their combined service adds up to a commendable 391 years. At just over the half century, Jim and Sarah still have some way to go. But really, after all this time, can the job still be interesting? Don't they ever feel they are living in aspic, maintaining a shard of a vanished world, as in the Wrest Park photograph?

They seem genuinely bemused by the question. Quoting one of Jim's heroes, John Sales, for twenty-five years chief gardens adviser to the National Trust, they point out that a garden is a process, constantly changing, that the joy of a garden is watching things grow and develop. That far from tending a museum piece, Sarah is in constant conference with commercial growers and serves on the RHS Fruit, Vegetable & Herb Committee, so there's a lively exchange of learning and innovation passing in and out of West Dean.

'If I ever do get up in the morning thinking, "not again",' muses Sarah, 'it's not the work that's the problem, but the back. Any frustrations are mostly the result of my own inadequacies and no one's fault but my own.'

She'd rather dwell on the positives – the way the beauty of the setting enriches and nourishes her, the freedom and security that come with working for a well-endowed foundation, rather than being subject to any individual's whim.

Above all, she relishes the stimulation of working in the creative artistic environment that West Dean provides – the college offers over seven hundred art-related courses. 'You get all these artists who come out and appreciate what you do, but from a variety of different perspectives. For example, there was a class this morning on texture – so you find yourself looking at your plants quite differently, and I love that. It gives me an excuse to grow whatever I fancy, however weird, because somebody will love it, someone will want to paint it or use it in some way. A student asked me yesterday if he could have a gourd, because they were once used for stringed instruments and he wants to have a go at making one. How wonderful is that?'

Jim, of course, concurs. 'The craft of gardening is about nurturing – nurturing plants, nurturing spaces – it's about loving something. It's difficult to love a computer . . . We are blessed to do something through which we are able to express our talents and our affections. How could you not love this place?'

He almost has a tear in his eye.

'Anyway, we couldn't possibly work anywhere else now,' says Sarah briskly. 'We're both far too long in the tooth.'

VISITOR INFORMATION

BROUGHTON GRANGE
Wykham Lane, Broughton, Banbury, Oxfordshire
OX15 5DS
Open every Wednesday from May to September,
10am–4pm
www.broughtongrange.com

GARDEN OF COSMIC SPECULATION
Portrack House, Holywood, Dumfries DG2 0RW
Portrack opens to the public just one afternoon a year
– check www.scotlandsgardens.org for details
www.charlesjencks.com

GREAT DIXTER
Northiam, Rye, East Sussex TN31 6PH
Open Tuesday to Sunday and bank holiday Mondays
from late March to October,
11am–5pm
www.greatdixter.co.uk

HEADLEY COURT
Headley Court is not open to the public

LOWTHER CASTLE
Penrith, Cumbria CA10 2HH
Open daily except Christmas Day, 10am–4pm
(winter) or 5pm (summer)
www.lowthercastle.org

MERTON COLLEGE
Merton Street, Oxford OX1 4JD
Open weekday afternoons and 10am–5pm at
weekends
www.merton.ox.ac.uk

PACKWOOD HOUSE
Packwood Lane, Lapworth, Warwickshire B94 6AT
Open Tuesday to Sunday and bank holiday and school
holiday Mondays, 11am–5pm. Closed Christmas Eve
and Christmas Day. In winter visits are by tour only –
check website for details
www.nationaltrust.org.uk/packwood-house

**ROOF GARDEN AT SOUTHBANK
CENTRE'S QUEEN ELIZABETH HALL**
Southbank Centre, Belvedere Road, London SE1 8XX
Garden and bar open daily from April to September,
10am–10pm
www.southbankcentre.co.uk

SISSINGHURST CASTLE GARDEN
Biddenden Rd, Cranbrook, Kent TN17 2AB
Open daily except for parts of January and March,
11am–5.30pm – check website for details. Closed
Christmas Eve and Christmas Day
www.nationaltrust.org.uk/sissinghurst-castle-garden

TRENTHAM GARDENS
The Trentham Estate, Stone Road, Trentham,
Stoke-on-Trent, Staffordshire ST4 8JG
Open daily except Christmas Day, 10am–4pm
(winter), later in summer – check website for details
www.trentham.co.uk

WALTHAM PLACE
Waltham Place, Church Hill, White Waltham,
Berkshire SL6 3JH
Visits by guided tour only – check website for details
www.walthamplace.com

WEST DEAN GARDENS
West Dean, near Chichester PO18 0RX
Open daily early February to late December –
check website for details
www.westdean.org.uk/gardens

THE WEIR
Swainshill, Hereford HR4 7QF
Open 11am–5pm daily late January to early
November. Additional weekend snowdrop openings in
January – check website for details
www.nationaltrust.org.uk/the-weir-garden

All gardens except Headley Court welcome group
visits by appointment.

INDEX

Page numbers in *italics* refer to illustrations.

ACKNOWLEDGEMENTS

I would like to thank all the gardeners and garden owners who have contributed to this project for their generosity in telling their stories and sharing their time and expertise, for their helpfulness, enthusiasm and inexhaustible patience. I began this book because I had been so impressed by various head gardeners I had met. A few years on, I can say with absolute conviction I never met a more admirable — or nicer — group of people.

I am grateful to Mike Calnan of the National Trust, John Watkins of English Heritage and Dominic Cole of the Gardens Trust for illuminating the bigger picture. I should also like to thank Jan Kingdom and Diana Ross for their helpful suggestions, Pia Östlund for giving polished form to our vague ramblings, Becky Clarke for her infinite forbearance and my brilliant editor Natasha Goodfellow for her elegance and skill. Huge thanks to my partner in crime Charlie Hopkinson, who in turn acknowledges his debt to Rosie Atkins and Claudia Zeff for setting him on the path of photographing gardeners.

Above all I thank Keith Auckland, who never got to see this book finished, but without whose unstinting help it could never have been written.